Key Strategies for Healthy Sunday Schools

A GUIDE FOR PASTORS, SUNDAY SCHOOL DIRECTORS,
MINISTERS OF EDUCATION, AND SUNDAY SCHOOL LEADERS

Compiled and Edited by
Dr. Steve Parr

Copyright © 2008 by the Georgia Baptist Convention, 6405 Sugarloaf Parkway, Duluth, GA 30097. All rights reserved. No part of this publication may be reproduced in any form, except for brief quotations in reviews, without permission from the publisher.

Published by Baxter Press, Friendswood, Texas
Graphic Design by Ardent Design, Decatur, Georgia
Printed in U.S.A.

ISBN #978-1-888237-80-1

KEY Strategies - FOR HEALTHY SUNDAY SCHOOLS

Acknowledgments

Key Strategies For Healthy Sunday Schools

We are all a compilation of everything we have read, heard, studied, learned, and discussed. We extend thanks to all who have influenced us in our leadership. We express a special word of gratitude and dedication to Andy Anderson and Harry Piland. These were men who loved God, served the church, and influenced us all to be better Sunday School leaders.

ABOUT THE AUTHORS

Steve Parr...
   is the Vice-President for Sunday School and Evangelism for the Georgia Baptist Convention.

Tim S. Smith...
   serves the Georgia Baptist Convention as Consultant and Team Coordinator for Sunday School/Open Group Ministries.

Earnie Burfitt...
   is the Minister of Education at Burnt Hickory Baptist Church in Marietta, Georgia.

Billy Britt...
   is the Pastor of Ministries at Hebron Baptist Church in Dacula, Georgia.

Keith Murdock...
   is the Minister of Adults at First Baptist Church in Duluth, Georgia.

Alan Folsom...
   serves the Georgia Baptist Convention as a Sunday School/Open Group Ministries Consultant.

Acknowledgments (continued)

John Yates...
> is the Minister of Education at Morningside Baptist Church in Valdosta, Georgia.

Bill Gambrell...
> is the Associate Pastor of Education and Program Ministries at Johnson Ferry Baptist Church in Marietta, Georgia.

Patrick Thompson...
> serves the Georgia Baptist Convention as a Sunday School/Open Group Ministries Consultant.

Table of Contents

Introduction   1

Key #1   3
Leaders Understand The Purpose Of Sunday School, By Tim S. Smith

Key #2   17
Sunday School Is Organized For Growth, By Earnie Burfitt

Key #3   29
Enrollment Is Properly Defined And Applied, By Billy Britt

Key #4   41
Contacts Are Made With Consistency, By Keith Murdock

Key #5   53
Leaders Are Trained For Effectiveness, By Steve Parr

Key #6   69
Teaching Is Relevant To the Audience, By Patrick Thompson

Key #7   79
Space Is Provided For Growth, By Alan Folsom

Key #8   95
There Is A Plan For Outreach, By John Yates

Key #9   107
New Units Are Created, By Bill Gambrell

Appendix   121
Georgia's Fastest Growing Sunday Schools: Ten Common Factors, By Dr. Steve Parr

KEY Strategies - FOR HEALTHY SUNDAY SCHOOLS

Introduction

What is the secret to Sunday School health and growth? The good news is that there is not a secret! There are principles at work that are timeless. Some methodologies can be contextualized and adapted to a variety of settings. But leaders of growing Sunday School ministries understand that there are principles that cannot be ignored if health and growth are the desired results.

The following pages contain nine keys that are based on principles that can unlock the potential of your Sunday School. These are described and discussed by proven leaders that have successfully guided their churches in effective Sunday School ministry. Each key is a strategic principle that is time-tested and remains relevant for the twenty-first century. The key strategies can be implemented in any church regardless of setting or size.

Each chapter is divided into four sections:
1. *Unlocking The Purpose Of…*
   The issue will be defined and discussed in the context of how it relates to Sunday School health.
2. *Finding The Right Combination*
   How should a church evaluate itself in relation to each particular key?
   What ratios are considered healthy (by age group where appropriate)?
3. *Breaking Through: How Healthy Sunday Schools Utilize…*
   How does the key strategy apply in a real world situation? How are churches utilizing the strategy to strengthen their Sunday School?
4. *Ten Key Ideas That You Can Use*
   Ten practical ideas are provided that can be used in churches of any size.

The concluding section of the book (the Appendix) contains research that summarizes the ten common factors of growing Sunday Schools.

Carefully consider these three points as you begin the study of the keys to growing a healthy Sunday School. First, none of the keys stands alone. Sunday Schools grow because they do many things well. The implementation and application of one or two keys without the others will not be sufficient to prompt or sustain growth.

Second, Sunday School growth takes work. Yes, it is first and foremost a work of God, but it is also the work of God through His body, the church. The ministry that occurs Monday through Saturday is as essential as the ministry that occurs on Sunday morning. These keys clearly make this point. Third, even healthy churches tend to struggle with one or more of these keys. These churches would humbly admit that they are still struggling with application and implementation of some of these strategies. There are no perfect churches, but there are churches passionate about reaching their communities and teaching God's Word. Take these key strategies and implement the principles and practical ideas to strengthen your Sunday School ministry!

KEY #1

LEADERS UNDERSTAND THE PURPOSE OF SUNDAY SCHOOL

Unlocking The Purpose of Sunday School
Get your keys! What is the most important key on your key ring? If your key ring is like mine then you have a pocket full of keys. I have three sets of car keys, keys to my office door, keys to my desk and file cabinets, a house key, and several more keys that I never actually use. On my dresser at home there are another three key rings that go to our camper, to other items in our home, and to the homes of friends and neighbors. Let me tell you a story about my most important key.

My family and I were returning from a week of vacation. It had been a good week of spending time with the family, but as you know that ride home can be long and tiring. This is especially true when it is hot and when you have young children in the car. You've heard it before. "Daddy, I need to go to the bathroom" within minutes after you had stopped for gas. "Are we there yet?" five minutes after they asked the last time. You get the picture. I was ready to get home! We pulled into the driveway and I was excited. I reached up to open the garage door but the garage door would not open. That is our way to get into the house. I got out of the car and discovered that the electricity was out in our neighborhood. Electric garage doors do not open without electricity! I made my way to the front door and reached into my pocket to pull out my keys to unlock the door. It was late at night, I was tired, I had been on the road and was ready to get to my bed. To my surprise there was no house key on my key ring! I looked at my wife and she said, "I gave it to the neighbors so they could get in to feed the dog and put up our mail." So I walked down the street to my neighbor's house to get my key. You guessed right. They were not at home!

I learned that night that the most important key on my key ring was the key to my house. I never used it because we always entered our house through the garage. I never thought about it! I took it for granted that I would always be able to get into my house, but when I really needed it, the house key was not there. That is how a lot of churches are today in their approach to Sunday School. They go through the motions and take for granted the purpose for providing a Sunday School ministry. They assume it will work as it is supposed to with little thought or attention.

Almost every Southern Baptist Church has a Sunday School or Small Group Bible Study ministry. On the surface they tend to appear to be the same. Most meet on Sunday morning prior to the worship service. They have a teacher, an assigned room, a generational grouping of members, and a Bible study. Although they appear to be doing the same thing they are not getting the same results. Some are alive and growing, while others are stagnant or declining. There is a difference when you get beneath the surface. One of the key differences is how they view the purpose of the Sunday School. The perceived purpose can be an energizer or a barrier. So what is the purpose of the Sunday School?

Finding The Right Combination

A historical view of the Sunday School is useful in understanding the real purpose of the Sunday School ministry. In his book, 21 Truths, Traditions & Trends, Bill Taylor gives an overview of the history of the Sunday School movement. There were many challenges faced by those wishing to do Great Commission work through the Sunday School. Taylor revisits some of those challenges in his historical summary.

Church historians do not agree on the date of the first Sunday School, but no one questions the contribution made by a young Englishman named Robert Raikes. His work with prisoners convinced him that religious education would keep young people out of jail. Because so many children worked in the factories every day except Sunday, he formed a school in 1780 that met on Sundays in the homes of lay teachers.

His first efforts were met with criticism on all fronts, especially from the clergy who seemed to be threatened by this new work. He and his schools were dubbed "Bobby Wildgoose and his ragged regiment." Within four years the first school in Gloucester had more than 250,000 children enrolled in Sunday School. By his death in 1811, the weekly Sunday School attendance had grown to more than 400,000.

William Elliott is credited with starting the first Sunday School in America. In 1785, he started a Bible study in his home. Sixteen years later, in 1801, the Sunday School was transferred to the Burton-Oak Grove Methodist Church in Brandfords Neck, Virginia. The second Sunday School was created in 1786, by Francis Asbury in the home of Thomas Crenshaw of Hanover County, Virginia. Its purpose was to provide religious education for the slaves on the plantations.

The news about this new way of sharing Bible truths and allowing people of all stations the privilege of studying the Word of God spread rapidly across America. The first national gathering of Sunday School leaders was held in Philadelphia in 1831, nearly 30 years after the first Sunday School was moved onto church property.

More than 119 years passed from the time Raikes started the first Sunday School until the first department specifically for adults was begun. It started in the Calvary Baptist Church of Washington, D.C. in 1899. W.A. Duncan noted the importance of this when he said, "There has been no thought or plan so important and so far reaching in its possibilities since the first Sunday School was organized."

One of the early Sunday School missionaries was Stephen Paxon. He is an example of a life considered of little value by the standards of the world, yet he moved from despair to triumph. Stephen was born crippled and had such a severe case of stuttering that when he was a child his peers called him "Stuttering Steve." His learning skills were so limited that he was denied the privilege of education, even in the primitive schools of his day. An unnamed Sunday School teacher reached out to Stephen and touched his life.

God moved in his heart, and Stephen dedicated his life to sharing the message of Jesus and fostering new Sunday Schools across America. Undaunted by bad weather, he exclaimed, "A Sunday School born in a snowstorm will never be scared by a white frost." He rode one horse, named Robert Raikes, for more than 25 years. It was said that the horse was so well trained that he would never pass a child on the road. The horse knew from Paxson's lifestyle that the missionary would stop to invite the child to Sunday School.

Paxon organized 1,314 new Sunday Schools, enrolling more than 83,000 in Bible study. He also encouraged the ongoing work of another 1,747 Sunday Schools. During one intensive period he organized 47 new Sunday Schools in 40 days.

Another man influential in the formation of the early Sunday School was Arthur Flake, a successful businessman. Once a traveling salesman, he entered the department store business in Winona, Mississippi, in 1894. He was the Sunday School Superintendent at Winona Baptist Church, and built his own Sunday School that became so successful it caught the attention of Mississippi Baptist leaders. In 1920 he went to work with the Baptist Sunday School Board and was charged with the task of developing Sunday School administration. Arthur Flake is credited with beginning what we today see as common. But his greatest contribution to Sunday School work lives on today and is foundational in all Sunday School work. It is known as *Flake's Formula* for Sunday School Growth.

1. Know the Possibilities
2. Enlist, Train and Motivate Workers
3. Provide the Space
4. Enlarge the Organization
5. Visit in the Name of the Lord

Taylor provides a more detailed historical overview in his book. In addition, there are many other leaders that could be mentioned for their contribution to Sunday School. In Ken Hemphill's book, <u>Revitalizing The Sunday Morning Dinosaur</u>, he rightly points out that the early architects of the Sunday School movement in America believed that the Sunday School must have a Great Commission focus. He states that they did not believe that the Sunday School could function properly without a clear and intentional strategy of evangelism. The pioneer leaders of Sunday School clearly understood the purpose of Sunday School.

> *"History reminds us that if the Sunday School and the church are going to be healthy, then great commitment and great sacrifice will be required."*

Those that are willing to pay the price understand why they do it, and they understand what needs to be done!

Ask a Sunday School leader or Sunday School member to share their understanding of the purpose of the Sunday School. They are likely to share something like this: "The purpose of the Sunday School is to study the Bible." The definition they share may or may not address any broader purpose. This definition is not incorrect but it is incomplete. Historically the purpose was centered on the study of the Bible with the ultimate aim of reaching people with the Gospel. What has happened to the evangelistic focus? Originally the Sunday School was focused on the Great

Commission and organized around the functions of the church as described in Acts 2:42-47. Meeting each week to study the Bible requires less energy, effort, and passion than actively engaging the class members in fulfilling the Great Commission. However, the Biblical and historical purpose cannot be accomplished by passively studying the Bible without regard to these roots.

The church today is failing to equip leaders and members to understand the purpose of the Sunday School. It is not only the responsibility of the Minister of Education, but also that of every leader. Pastors, Ministers of Music, Ministers of Students, Sunday School Directors, Preschool teachers, Children's teachers, Youth teachers, Adult teachers, Department Directors, and class members alike must know and understand the purpose of the Sunday School. If the correct purpose is not communicated and understood, today's church members will not be as willing to pay the price as the men described by Bill Taylor.

In the book, <u>Kingdom Principles for Church Growth</u>, Gene Mims develops the 1-5-4 Principle. This is the foundational starting point for understanding the purpose of Sunday School.

1- The driving force for the church must be … The Great Commission
5- The functions of the church …
- Evangelism
- Discipleship
- Fellowship
- Ministry
- Worship

4- The results will be …
- Numerical Growth
- Spiritual Growth
- Ministries Expansion
- Missions Advance

This is a biblically based model of what the church is to be! The next questions are "how" and "what's the plan?" This is where the Sunday School fits into the picture. The Sunday School permits the church to strategically organize and focus the church on the Great Commission and the five key functions. The historical perspective of Sunday School affirms this point.

Finding the right combination for developing and communicating the purpose of the Sunday School must be based on the following:

1. The purpose must be consistent with the call of the Great Commission.
2. The purpose must comprehensively engage class members in the functions of the church.

Breaking Through: How Healthy Sunday Schools Utilize the Purpose of Sunday School

What do the following churches have in common?
- A church that does not provide training or encourage leaders to participate in training,
- A church that purges the Sunday School rolls of those that do not attend,
- A church that is resistant to creating new classes,
- A church that does not emphasize the involvement of adults in Sunday School,
- A church that focuses on Worship growth without regard to Sunday School growth,
- A church that does not organize care groups in the Sunday School,
- A church whose pastor does not support the Sunday School,
- A church that has three times as much worship space as education space,
- A church that does not organize or reorganize the Sunday School regularly.

The common factor among these churches is that they do not understand or communicate the purpose of the Sunday School.

"Sunday School is the foundational strategy in a local church for leading people to faith in the Lord Jesus Christ and for building Great Commission Christians through Bible study groups that engage people in evangelism, discipleship, fellowship, ministry and worship." This is the definition of Sunday School from the book Sunday School for a New Century by Bill Taylor and Louis Hanks. It is with this definition that we make the connection of missions and the purpose of Sunday School and church.

"Sunday School is not just another organization of the church. It is the church organized for growth and ministry."

Sunday School is more than the Bible teaching ministry of the church. Sunday School is not just another organization of the church. It is the church organized for growth and ministry. Sunday School is the church doing the work of the church. Sunday School is a seven-day-a-week-twenty-four-hour-a-day strategy, not a one-day-a-week-in-one-hour meeting. These are the elements that must be understood by the leadership and should also be part of the purpose/mission statement for your Sunday School.

There is a proverb that states: "If you aim at nothing, you will hit it every time." The development and communication of a stated purpose is essential to insure that your Sunday School is on target for months and years into the future. Jesus told His disciples in Matthew 28:19-20a: "Go therefore and make disciples of all nations, baptizing them in the name of the Father and of the Son and of the Holy Spirit, teaching them to observe all things I have commanded you." Jesus gave his followers a clear purpose that the church holds dear to this day. This Great Commission remains the standard and is a key motivation for all that the church is called to do.

How about your Sunday School? What is the purpose of your Sunday School? Does your Sunday School have a clear purpose? It was the vision of Christopher Columbus returning to Spain with ships full of spices, converts, and gold that led Queen Isabella to grant him the funds for his journey. She surely would not have granted him the funds if he had approached her with "I need three ships, lots of men, lots of time, and maybe I'll get back to you." Columbus provided Queen Isabella with a clear picture of what could be accomplished if the necessary resources were in place. Likewise, a clearly communicated purpose for your Sunday School can serve as a verbal picture to clearly show your members and leaders why your Sunday School exists! Do you meet because it is expected? Do you meet because it is a tradition? Do you meet because it is the "Baptist" thing to do? In order for a Sunday School Ministry to be on target there must be a clearly communicated vision and purpose.

Developing and communicating the purpose of your Sunday School ministry with a clear Purpose Statement will help keep your church on target in several ways. First of all, a Purpose Statement is a directional instrument; it will serve as a compass to insure that your Small Group Bible Study is moving in the right direction. Should your Sunday School be aimed towards fellowship? Ministry to the membership? New members? Mature disciples? Or a combination of several factors? There are dozens of possible answers. However, if you try to move in many directions, you may not move at all. A Purpose Statement will help to point all of your classes in a common direction. Second, a Purpose Statement is a lens. You can look at all you do in Sunday School through this lens. This will help your church to discern where to place their time, priorities, and resources. Discerning whether to say "yes" or "no" to the good things and the best things will be clearer when viewed through this lens. Third, a Purpose Statement serves as a measuring stick. It can serve as a tool to help you evaluate how your Sunday School is doing. Rick Warren says that successful leaders ask two key questions each week. First of all, "what is our business?" and second, "How's business?" A Purpose Statement will help your church address these same questions. Why do you have Sunday School? Your Purpose Statement will get to the heart of this question!

Keep the following points in mind as you consider the development of a Purpose Statement for your Sunday School. First, this is only a beginning point. You must consider how to organize around that purpose and to strategically implement a ministry that will fulfill the stated purpose. Second, not just any purpose will do! A wrongly defined or poorly communicated purpose can become a barrier in the same way that a rightly defined and communicated purpose can be a motivation.

Ten Key Ideas That You Can Use

1. *Apply the Great Commission.* Your church already believes the Great Commission as a command from Christ. Use the Great Commission, Matthew 28:18-20, as the stated purpose of the Sunday School. Any purpose must be consistent with the Great Commission. Christ compels the church to "make disciples." Notice that He uses three verbs in this context. They are "go," "baptize," and "teach." The principles of evangelizing, assimilating, and teaching are grouped together.

2. *Adopt the definition from* **Sunday School For A New Century**. This definition is consistent with the Great Commission and focuses each class comprehensively on all of the functions of the church. The definition is as follows: *Sunday School is the foundational strategy in a local church for leading people to faith in the Lord Jesus Christ and for building Great Commission Christians through Bible study groups that engage people in evangelism, discipleship, fellowship, ministry, and worship.* This can serve very well as a Purpose Statement for your Sunday School.

3. *Survey your Sunday School leaders.* Ask each of your leaders to write a response to the following statement: "The purpose of the Sunday School at _____ Baptist Church is…" This response will help you evaluate the understanding that your leaders have of the purpose of Sunday School.

4. *Survey your Sunday School members.* Ask the same question of those that attend your Sunday School. Are their answers consistent with those of the leaders? Is their understanding of the purpose consistent with the Great Commission and the functions of the church?

5. *Schedule a Realignment Sunday.* This is a special Sunday to focus the entire congregation on the purpose of the Sunday School. Plan activities for worship as well as the small group time to realign all of the members with the correct purpose of Sunday School.

6. *Post the purpose in all classes.* Keep the purpose of the Sunday School in the mind of all Sunday School members by posting your Purpose Statement in each class. This should be placed in an area that is seen by everyone each Sunday. Keep the purpose posted at all times!

7. *Print the purpose in bulletins and mail outs.* Refresh and remind people why your Sunday School exists by printing the purpose in written materials that are viewed by a wide range of the congregation. Do this on a frequent basis.

8. *Print bookmarks with the Purpose Statement.* Encourage members to place a bookmark in their Bibles to remind them of the purpose of the Sunday School in your church.

9. *Have the leaders memorize the Purpose Statement.* Challenge and encourage Sunday School leaders to know the Purpose Statement by memory.

10. *Develop a personalized Purpose Statement for your church.* The concluding section provides a plan for your church to accomplish this task. This is strongly recommended for each church.

A Detailed Process For Developing A Personalized Purpose Statement

It is not your job to create the purposes of the church (Sunday School) but to discover them. How can you discover the purpose of your Sunday School? The best results will be born out of a process involving several people committed to prayer, study of God's Word, and the desire to partner together to discover this purpose. Here, then, is the process.

Step 1 – Enlistment of a Team

The Purpose Statement Team will be enlisted to work together to seek God in the development of a Purpose Statement for the Sunday School.

The team should be composed of six to twelve members. Each member should be a committed participant in the Sunday School Ministry. The team should include:
- 1-2 Staff Members
- 2-4 Sunday School Teachers (from various age groups)
- 2-4 Sunday School Members (from various age groups)
- 1-2 Sunday School Officers (Directors, Outreach Leaders, Care Group Leaders, Etc.)

Try to develop a good cross-section from the congregation. Are there males and females on the team? Are there married adults and single adults? Are all generations represented (Senior Adults, Median Adults, and Young Adults)? Are there staff members and volunteers?

Who will be the Team Captain? He/She will begin providing leadership at Step 2 (or with the enlistment of the team if desired).

Step 2 – Determine a Meeting Schedule

The team should plan to meet for six weeks in a row. Each meeting should last approximately one hour. When will the team meet? Where will the team meetings be held? Who will reserve the room? Who will type and publish the schedule for the team members?

Step 3 – Orientation Session (First Meeting)

The first session should accomplish the following:
- Members should be introduced. Have each member share about their relationship to Sunday School.

- The leader should discuss the purpose of the Purpose Statement Team.
- Time should be spent in prayer.
- The meeting schedule should be previewed.
- Members will be given the first assignment:
    Study what the Bible says about the purpose of the church.
    Look for answers to four questions:
    1. *Why does the church exist?*
    2. *What are we to be as a church? (Who and what are we?)*
    3. *What are we to do as a church? (What does God want us to do?)*
    4. *How are we to do the work of the church?*
    Study Matthew 28:19-20, Acts 2:42-47, and at least two other passages that God puts on your heart. Write down your thoughts and bring these to the next session.

Step 4 – Discovery Session (Second Meeting)

This purpose of this session is to compile a summary of the team's findings during their time of study. Each person should be encouraged to take two to four minutes to share his or her results. A recorder should write key phrases on a board or a sheet of poster paper.

The balance of the time should be given to the discussion of these questions: Which of these principles apply specifically to Sunday School? Which do not?

Challenge each member to spend at least two hours in prayer prior to the next session.

Step 5 – Concepts Session (Third Meeting)

This purpose of this session is to summarize concepts that apply to the purpose of Sunday School.
- Begin with a time of prayer and a review of the previous meetings.
- Give each member ten index cards. Ask each member to do the following:
    Take the next twenty minutes to think through your studies and our discussions about the biblical purposes of Sunday School. Without talking or conferring with other team members, write concepts, words, or phrases that you think describe the purpose of the Sunday School. Write only one concept, word, or phrase on each card. Each team member was given ten cards. However, you may write as few or as many as God places on your heart. More cards are available if needed.

KEY Strategies - FOR HEALTHY SUNDAY SCHOOLS

- At the conclusion of this time, lay all of the cards "face up" on the table(s). Work as a team to place cards that have similar words, phrases, and concepts into individual stacks.
- Give each stack a label that describes the key concept found in the responses.
- Work as a team to arrange the stacks in the order of their priority or purpose. Work together to agree on the most important three to six concepts.

Step 6 - Defining Session (Fourth Meeting)
This purpose of this session is to begin the development of a written Purpose Statement for your Sunday School.
- Spend time together in prayer.
- Continue to work on any unfinished items from the previous session.
- Work as a team to write a short paragraph summarizing the purpose of your Sunday School in the context of the agreed upon concepts from the previous exercises. Rewrite it two or three times to sharpen up the wording. The paragraph should begin with: *"The purpose of our Sunday School is . . ."*
- Next, eliminate as many unnecessary words and phrases as possible.

Step 7 – Writing the Purpose Statement (Fifth Meeting)
An effective Purpose Statement will have the following characteristics:
1. It should be no more than one sentence long.
2. It should be easily understood by a twelve year old.
3. It should be able to be recited by memory on demand.

What to do in this meeting…
- Spend time together in prayer.
- Work together to narrow the brief paragraph to a single sentence. Begin with: "The purpose of the _____ Baptist Church Sunday School is . . ."
- Fine tune, edit, and work with it. Keep the three characteristics above in mind.
- Rejoice and thank God!
- Discuss ways to communicate the Purpose Statement with the congregation.

Step 8 – Completion and Celebration (Sixth Meeting)
This meeting is scheduled to give the team additional time to complete the task if needed and/or to celebrate the completion of the development phase of the Purpose Statement for Sunday School.

Sample Sunday School Purpose Statements

"The Sunday School of _____ Baptist Church is to TEACH the Bible to change lives, REACH the lost with the Good News of Jesus and CARE for people through prayer, ministry and fellowship."

"At _____ Baptist Church the Bible study groups are PEOPLE experiencing life changing Bible study and engaging in a lifestyle of reaching and serving others for JESUS CHRIST with a group of genuine friends."

The Promotion of Your Developed Purpose

Your Purpose Statement will focus your ministry on what you want it to be (character) or to do (contributions) and on the values or principles upon which being and doing are based. The final step in developing your Purpose Statement is to communicate this purpose with your leaders and congregation so that they will clearly understand the value and the purposes of your Sunday School Ministry. Why should our members be committed if they do not understand what they are committing to? This communication can be accomplished in several ways:

- Have posters printed and displayed to communicate the new Purpose Statement.
- Print the Purpose Statement in the bulletin in the following weeks.
- Post the Purpose Statement in each Sunday School class.
- Challenge each Sunday School leader to memorize the Purpose Statement.
- Develop Bible study lessons on the new Purpose Statement. Ask every teacher to teach the statement in their class.
- Post the Purpose Statement on bulletin boards in hallways.
- Have the pastor preach a sermon to emphasize the purpose of your Sunday School.
- Use the Purpose Statement in all leadership meetings for planning and evaluation.
- Print the Purpose Statement on all church publications.
- Ask the Banner ministry leaders in your church to develop a banner using the Purpose Statement.
- Develop a Sunday School leader training event keyed to providing ideas to assist each age group in fulfilling the Purpose Statement.

Remember how this chapter began? It began with my experience of being locked out of my house at night, after a long trip, with a non-working garage door opener and no way to get my house key. I never finished the story. How do you think I got in? That is right. I got in by a way that cost me later. Don't make the same mistake with your Sunday School. Don't let inattention to this ministry cost you later. Develop the Purpose Statement, communicate the Purpose Statement to your congregation and use it as a guide in your enlistment, training, planning and evaluation of your Sunday School.

Thanks to Bill Taylor, Gene Mims, Ken Hemphill and Steve Parr for the ideas used in this section.

KEY #2

SUNDAY SCHOOL IS ORGANIZED FOR GROWTH

Unlocking The Purpose of Organization

When you think of how your Sunday School is put together– how it is organized– do the words efficient and effective come to mind? The need for an organizational strategy is almost as old as Sunday School itself. In the past, this strategy was called a "grading plan" because Sunday School was mostly for children of school age. Today, Sunday School is, or should be, designed for all ages. Through the years, Sunday School leaders have seen the value of good Sunday School organization. In Building a Standard Sunday School, Arthur Flake says, "If a Sunday School is properly graded [organized], it is possible to have everything else of value to make the Sunday School efficient." One of our contemporary leaders, Ken Hemphill, champions the importance of Sunday School in his book Revitalizing the Sunday Morning Dinosaur. He states "an effective organizational plan places the resources of the church at the full disposal of the Lord that they might be used in the most efficient manner for the fulfillment of the Great Commission."

Sunday School is the only group within the church that is challenged to help the church fulfill all of the functions spelled out in the New Testament. An organized Sunday School can help the church to more:

1. *Efficiently Reach and Evangelize*: Organizing Sunday School around those things that members and prospects have in common makes the reaching task happen more naturally. People naturally share and open up with those with whom they have something in common. If they have children a certain age, they will be attracted to others with children that age. Couples who are engaged tend to know more people who are engaged, and so on. Organizing the Sunday School, particularly for adults, can make reaching others more effective by giving members a common bond that they can share with others who are not involved in Bible Study. Within the class, proper organization assures that prospects are not left out of the loop or do not fall through the cracks.

2. *Effectively Teach and Disciple*: Through the use of a good organizational plan, the Sunday School can accomplish the aim of teaching and making disciples. People learn in a variety of ways. Many of these differences are generational. Experience shows that many older adults prefer a more structured learning environment while many younger adults prefer more interactive learning. Children learn based on skill and knowledge levels; a two year-old child cannot work a word puzzle and a ten year-old child will be bored with a six piece wooden puzzle. Throughout the Sunday School, organization can make teaching, learning, and discipling more effective.

3. *Easily Minister*: Again, the factor of common ground works to your advantage when organizing for ministry. As a church grows, it becomes harder for the pastor and staff to touch everyone who has a ministry need. In addition, based on Ephesians 4, it is not the sole responsibility of the pastor or the staff to do the ministering; the members are to "do the work of the ministry." By dividing the church into small groups and giving members responsibility for those groups, the church can more easily minister to every member. This is the same advice that Moses got from Jethro in Exodus 18:18. "The work is too heavy for you," he said, "you cannot handle it alone." In essence, Jethro's advice to his son-in-law was, "Get organized, son!" As Sunday School is the church divided into small groups, so is Sunday School divided into smaller care groups. Creating care groups within the adult and youth classes produces the same type of sub-structure as the Sunday School within the church. By utilizing class care groups, needs of the members can be discovered and met.

4. *Effortlessly Fellowship*: Common ground helps to build the sense of community and family that should be a part of every church. As the world grows technologically, it also grows more sterile. Rick Warren says, "People are not looking for a friendly church, they are looking for friends." Organizing small groups around some common ground allows people to develop the relationships that make for great fellowship. Or is it the fellowship that makes for great friendships? Or is it both?

5. *Enthusiastically Worship*: Through age and skill level appropriate teaching, church members can learn the meaning and value of personal worship. Consider what would happen to your worship services if the members of the church purposefully spent time with God throughout the week? What would happen if God met their needs through the ministry of the church? How would worship be different

if they have celebrated and shared together what God has done in their lives? What kind of worship service would you experience?

Finding the Right Combination

How do you determine what common factors to use when organizing the Sunday School? Any system could work but many would end up getting the Sunday School leadership lynched. Try grading the women by weight. Or the men by I.Q. Either way you would be in trouble! Organizing by age is simple and makes the most sense for the participants' education and maturity level. Six-year-old children have the same basic needs and skills as other six year-olds, but they have little in common with sixteen or sixty year-olds. The sixty year-old will have more common ground with older median age adults than he or she will have with a twenty year-old newlywed.

You need to have an awareness of the most effective ratios of leaders to learners. These ratios vary based on the age of the audience. View the ratios as "rules of thumb" rather than "laws." A larger congregation will tend to have slightly larger ratios. The rules of thumb can be stretched. However, as you stray further from the recommended ratios you are also likely to struggle with effectiveness in discipling and ministering to that particular age group. Most growing churches have a ratio of about one class for every twenty to twenty-two enrolled in Sunday School for all age groups combined. Younger classes will generally need to be smaller classes. You might get by with a class attendance of twenty-five adults, but that probably is not wise for a two year-old class. You will generally have few issues if you have a couple of larger classes, but if all of the classes are large you will find that your leaders will struggle with ministry to all of their members. When is a class too large?

- When the teacher does not know each member personally.
- When the group is too large to have discussion.
- When the room is filled to capacity on a regular basis.
- When fewer than forty percent attend in a class where recommended enrollment is exceeded (This is an indication that the leader cannot manage ministry of that number of people).

The following are the recommended guidelines for organizing your Sunday School.

PRESCHOOL

Each class or group of preschoolers is considered a department within itself. The recommended number of leaders reflects the needs of the preschoolers. No department should have fewer than two workers. The maximum enrollment figures may be adjusted downward if the rooms are too small. Many churches wisely adopt policies concerning who may work with preschoolers. Some policies are simply common sense for the safety of the children, and they give the Sunday School leadership direction when placing workers. Other policies are due to the litigious nature of today's culture. For example, churches may require that leaders be at least eighteen years old to work with preschoolers. Other policies may restrict men from changing diapers or may insist that there is always a woman in the room if there is a male teacher. In the past, many of these types of policies may have been unnecessary, but today they give parents a sense of security about the care of their preschoolers. Be sure that your leadership has a working knowledge of current legal issues in order to provide the best protection for your children and your church.

GROUPING PRESCHOOLERS		
Age	**Maximum Enrollment**	**Leader: Learner Ratio**
Babies	12	1:2
Ones – Twos	12	1:3
Threes – Pre-K	16	1:4
Kindergarten	20	1:5

CHILDREN AND YOUTH

It is best if children and youth are grouped by their grade level in school rather than by their age. Like the Preschool, the Children's Sunday School should be organized into departments, with each class being a separate department. Again, the room size may be the limiting factor in determining the maximum number of children per class. Each class of children should have a minimum of two workers.

Youth should be organized into both departments and classes. Each Sunday School should determine whether they want guys and girls together in the youth department(s). Where possible, make divisions by school grade or by middle and high school. Each class of young people needs a minimum of two adult leaders. This provides support for the leaders and a further example for the teenagers. Other leaders for youth departments might include an outreach coordinator, a department director, and secretary. Again, some common sense guidelines when selecting workers will make the parents and the students comfortable and will enhance the teaching and learning environments.

GROUPING CHILDREN AND YOUTH		
Age	Maximum Enrollment	Leader: Learner Ratio
Grades 1-6	24	1:6
Grades 7-12	24	1:8

ADULTS

Organizing adults can be challenging but doing so affords tremendous value to the effectiveness of the ministry. Should the adult classes be age graded?

> *"Age grading provides a natural way of identifying affinity for most adults."*

The purpose of age grading is to help new members assimilate by making it easy to identify where other adults attend who are in a similar life stage. Ken Hemphill says, "You organize the adults based on who you want to reach rather than on who attends." Adult classes should be age graded to assist guests in finding their place as well as for providing accountability for outreach and follow-up. Providing classes by decade (example: thirties, forties, fifties, etc.) may remove some of the pressure from someone having to give their specific age.

Another factor that may enhance the effectiveness of the organization is to take into account the children of adults. Parents of preschoolers have many things in common regardless of their age. Some adults may feel a closer bond with those in similar life stages than with those who are simply the same age. Don't be afraid to post the age target of the class on the door and/or in written materials. But, what do you do if the members of the class do not reflect the publicized age grouping? You change the sign on the door. And if needed you start a new class to reach any age group not represented. Many Sunday Schools stagnate because they refuse to address this issue through regular reorganization and/or realignment of adult classes. The result of leaving everything alone will be a Young Married Class with couples in their forties (or even older). The consequence that follows is that you find it difficult to reach and assimilate new young married couples. Churches often wait so long to realign Adult Sunday School classes that few, if any, young adults attend at all.

KEY Strategies - FOR HEALTHY SUNDAY SCHOOLS

Each department should have a leader to learner ratio of at least 1:12. However, maximum effectiveness in ministry will require more leaders. Strive to get the ratio as close to 1:5 as possible and you will see an incredible difference. Those included in this ratio would be all class members with leadership assignments including roles such as class secretaries, care group leaders, outreach/ evangelism leaders, and departmental leadership. This will give several adults the opportunity to exercise their gifts and will insure an adequate number of care group and outreach leaders.

Adult classes should always be open to new members. A closed class is one that begins to exist solely to meet the needs of those who attend whether by choice or tradition. There was a men's class in a local church that went out and bought recliners for chairs in their classroom, one recliner for each man on roll. How would you feel if you visited that class and everyone had a recliner but you where given a folding chair? By thinking of their own comfort, they almost certainly eliminated the possibility of reaching anyone new. They became a closed class. Getting into a study that builds on itself from week to week can close other classes. For example, Henry Blackaby's book, Experiencing God, is wonderful. However, it would be almost impossible for a new member to pick up the study several weeks into it. By selecting a curriculum piece like Experiencing God, the class closes itself off from reaching new members.

	GROUPING ADULTS	
Age	Maximum Enrollment	Leader: Learner Ratio
***	30	1:12

***Aim for age spans of ten years or less and avoid age spans of more than fifteen years.

For more information about organizing by age group, see Ten Best Practices To Make Your Sunday School Work: page 77.

Breaking Through: How Healthy Sunday Schools Utilize Organization

Sunday School strategy is implemented by clustering people into groups, primarily on the basis of age. Remember, however, Sunday School is not an organization, but a strategy for doing the work of the Great Commission.

The individual classes are where the personal touch takes place. It is where people are mobilized to do the work. The importance of the organizational unit cannot be overemphasized.

Sunday School For A New Century

An adequately organized Sunday School maximizes the potential of the church for fulfilling its calling and purpose. Dependence on one individual in a class, or a small group of individuals in a church, will not reach the potential that a team of people will.

In his book <u>Redefining Church Membership – from Myth to Ministry</u>, John Powers talks about climbers attempting an ascent on the summit of Mount Everest. He says:

> *The point is, whether they are inexperienced amateurs or world-class veterans of the peak, for obvious reasons a mountaineer is rarely left alone on the face of Everest. The odds of surviving a push to the snow-capped summit of Everest improve greatly when a trekker surrounds himself or herself with a team of people committed to the same goal.*

Just as the mountain climber needs a team to reach the top, members within the church need to use the gifts and skills of the entire membership in order to be successful. In the book of Acts, over-dependence on a small group of leaders in the early church led to complaints. Spreading the responsibilities out over a larger group built unity in the church and helped the church to continue growing. The New Testament illustrates this team concept with a picture of the human body. In discussing the body, the apostle Paul gives us a ridiculous illustration of the whole body being an eye. Stop and let that image come to mind. It looks like something from a comic book does it not? Just as the human body is not made up of only an eye, the Sunday School cannot be a one-man-band. Congregations as well as individual Sunday School classes must utilize the gifts of all the members. Dividing and sharing the work among the members of the class or congregation strengthens all members and ministries.

The need for individuals to grow and be involved in fulfilling their calling is another aspect of organization. In his book, <u>When God Builds a Church</u>, Bob Russell says, "If your church [or class] is not providing opportunities for your members to serve, you are stifling their spiritual growth." Each member of the body is gifted for a place of service within the body. The church or class that is dependent on a small group of leaders to do all of the work robs the other members of the opportunity for ministry.

In <u>Ten Best Practices to make your Sunday School Work</u>, Ken Hemphill lists seven positive effects of a good organizational strategy. A good organizational strategy will:
1. Enable the church to fulfill the Great Commission.
2. Serve as a master plan and thus help avoid costly missteps.
3. Enable a church to manage its resources.
4. Create a team spirit.
5. Provide for better communication.
6. Help explain the creation of new units.
7. Enhance the total ministry of the church.

In addition, a good organizational strategy:
- Provides an opportunity for members to discover and develop their spiritual gifts.
- Assures that members' needs are discovered and met.
- Aids in the application of Scripture to the lives of members and prospects.

Continued growth is the main reason for putting an organizational strategy into place. The creation of additional classes will provide the framework needed to continue to reach new people and to assimilate them into the life of the congregation. If all leaders understand that there is a reason and a strategy for limiting the size of classes and departments, the creation of new classes will go much more smoothly. Remind leaders that new classes can better meet the needs of the members and provide an opportunity for growth. Churches celebrate when one of their members is called into missions. Why not celebrate as a class when a group is called out to go to the deepest darkest regions of the room across the hall? Let the existing class become like a home church for those who are going out on mission to start a new class.

Other opportunities for new classes come when unmet needs are discovered. Unmet needs may include an age group or life stage group that is not represented by the current organizational strategy. As existing classes mature, you may discover the need for a young married class. If you have a good number of college students, a nearly and newly married class might be a way of expanding the organization and reaching a new group of people.

> *"As you evaluate your Sunday School, ask the question" whom are we missing?" The answer might be a new class just waiting to be started.*

(See Chapter Eight for greater detail and help in starting new classes)

Ten Key Ideas That You Can Use

1. *Ask the Lord for guidance as you lead the Sunday School.* This may seem simple or obvious when it is actually the most critical step in organizing the church to carry out the Great Commission. God gave Moses the skills he needed to organize the children of Israel. He gave Paul the words to write to help organize the New Testament churches. He will guide you if you are seeking to build His kingdom.

2. *Adopt Sunday School as the strategy of the church to carry out the Great Commission.* No other group in the church is charged with all of the purposes of the church. While this may seem as easy as point number one, it is not any less important. The better the church understands the role of Sunday School, the more effective the church will be in building a Great Commission body.

3. *Assess the needs of the church when establishing the organizational strategy.* Create an age profile of your church. Either by hand or with the help of a computer, outline the ages of the members by decades or in five-year increments. By charting this data you will get a picture of what your organization may need to look like. If, for example, you see that you have forty-six married adults between the ages of forty and sixty-five you will know that you need at least two classes in this age group. If you want to be in the best position to grow, make three smaller classes and give them room to reach others.

4. *Approve an organizational plan that both limits the size of classes and encourages the creation of new classes.* When you take your organizational plan to the church, tell them what your ideal class would look like. Show them what kind of circumstances will trigger the formation of new classes. Good communication, high expectations, and enthusiastic support will help the church catch your vision for a growing, maturing congregation.

5. *Assemble a good team. Seek out the best individuals you can to be the leaders of your Sunday School ministry.* Ask for and expect the very best out of those you recruit. Ask your leaders what the Lord and the church should expect from a Sunday School leader. You will be surprised how high a standard they will set for themselves. Let their list be your standard for excellence. You may even want this list of expectations to be your worker covenant. Recruit your teachers of adults with the expectation of duplicating themselves and sending out workers into the harvest.

6. *Age grade classes for effective teaching and learning.* Age grading with children and youth is a no-brainer. It is natural to organize them by their natural stage of development. Recruiting adequate leadership for the number of classes that you need may be a more difficult task. But, the task is worth the effort! The same holds true for your adults. The task is worth it! Seek out the obvious leaders in the church. Explain the needs and the benefits of organizing adults into smaller units with age and life stage as the point of commonality. Enlist their support and begin to plan for those you will reach as you move forward.

7. *Assist class leaders in organizing their class.* Maybe your Sunday School is well organized. The next step is to make sure each youth and adult class is organized for ministry and growth. Visit Lifeway.com or ssog.gabaptist.com for job descriptions for various leadership roles. Seek to move each class into care groups. Encourage class leaders to hold their care group leaders accountable. Remember Jesus words: "You have not because you ask not."

8. *Assimilate new church members by providing a place for them in each class.* Adopt a policy of assigning (enrolling) all new members to a Sunday School class. This means that you must also have the policy of classes being open to new members. It is sometimes hard to break into a new group. It should not be hard to get into a Sunday School class. Ask for and expect each class to be open to guests and new members. If one is not open to growth, start a new class for the same age grouping and let the old one be left in the dust. An old farmer once said that you can dynamite a stump out of the ground but sometimes it is not worth the mess you have to clean up. If you have a class that refuses to accept new members, share with them the church's plan and expectations. If they still refuse, you may have to plow around them.

9. *Ask leaders to watch for opportunities to expand the organizational structure.* Your best source of information about new class possibilities, other than your age profile, is the teacher in the class. They can tell you if any natural divisions have occurred in the class that might lead to a new class. They can also tell you the general ages of the guests who have visited the class. Have them inform you when they have a member that is ready to take on a leadership role. Encourage class leaders to seek out ways to begin new classes. Remind your adult teachers that all leaders come from adult Sunday School classes. Be sure to recognize classes that do a good job of releasing members to serve in other areas of ministry.

10. *Annually review the effectiveness of the organizational structure.* Plan a time each year when you will take a critical look at your organizational structure. Begin with the preschool. Do you have an adequate number of classes and workers? Has that influx of students in your youth class been mostly from the middle school? Could you create two new classes where only one was necessary last year? Did the last member of the Young Married class just turn forty? Maybe it is time for a "younger" Young Married class. Look also at what classes are working well. Are the classes organized and ministering to the members? If not you may need to spend some extra time encouraging those leaders. It is less stressful to make small adjustments annually than to fail to implement any reorganization and later attempt to make a major overhaul of the ministry. Make adjustments every year, particularly as the new Sunday School year begins.

KEY #3

ENROLLMENT IS PROPERLY DEFINED AND APPLIED

Unlocking the Purpose of Enrollment

What is the key to Sunday School growth? Pastors and Sunday School leaders that have found success consistently point to growth in enrollment as key to Sunday School growth. Sunday School enrollment, when understood and used properly, is absolutely crucial to developing a healthy Sunday School. Enrollment impacts the attendance in Sunday School in the same manner that a thermostat affects the temperature of a room. Attendance will always follow and conform to the direction of enrollment. There is no way to sustain an increase in attendance while declining in enrollment. An increasing enrollment is essential to growing the Sunday School attendance. Additionally, enrollment affects other aspects of the church. An increasing enrollment will also increase baptisms, increase the number of leaders, as well as increasing the budget and other essential ministries. Properly utilizing your Sunday School enrollment is the key to unlocking the potential for growth in your Sunday School.

Dr. Ken Hemphill has written an excellent book on Sunday School growth entitled <u>Revitalizing the Sunday Morning Dinosaur</u>. In the book he speaks to the importance of focusing on Sunday School enrollment:

> Every church struggles with the leaks that allow people to drop out of involvement without being noticed. The problem increases as the church grows in numerical size. I can still remember staff meetings when someone would ask about a particular family. As we discussed their needs, we would realize that no one has seen them recently. When the task is assumed to be the responsibility of everyone, it becomes the concern of no one. By the time we made the contact, the situation that had led to their inactivity had often escalated to the point of no return. We knew we had to have a more systematic and comprehensive way to assure that everyone was cared for. This led to our strategy for universal enrollment, a plan for enrolling every church member in a small group for assimilation, Bible study, and discipleship.

Dr. Thom Rainer, in his book <u>High Expectations</u>, shares the results of a study of two thousand churches of all denominations that were growing. In his research of high growth and high assimilation churches, he discovered that all of them had focused on Sunday School as a primary outreach and assimilation tool. He says:

> *But the mere existence of a Sunday School does not produce assimilation. The classes must have the best and most thoroughly trained teachers. Expectations must be clear that ministry and evangelism should take place within each class. And the organization itself should be well run with good records [enrollment] and strong administrative leaders. Sunday School works. But only if we work Sunday School.*

Long time church growth leader and Sunday School advocate Dr. Elmer Towns has produced a training course entitled Sunday School Enrollment: Reviving a New Testament Strategy of Outreach. In chapter 3 of the training manual he says that Sunday School enrollment began to die out years ago when pastors and Christian educators began to emphasize the credibility of attendance rather than enrollment. Many felt that enrollment was just a bloated record since many on the roll did not actually attend regularly. He says:

> *An effective effort was made to pare the roll down to those who actually attended rather than using the roll as a pool from which to draw prospects or visitors. While this was intended to more accurately reflect church attendance, it indirectly contributed to an attendance decline. Attendance suffered because marginal members [those not on the roll] were neglected. Enrolling new members was not emphasized because all energy was placed on attendance. The enrollment "window of entry" was lost to the Sunday School. The church was left with one less way of reaching people.*

Dr. Towns further points out that when enrollment is emphasized it requires classes to take responsibility for individuals in their group. It encourages members to be concerned about the spiritual health of his or her friends. Enrollment opens a new "window of entry" to invite people into the church.

"Mr. Sunday School" for Southern Baptists for years was Dr. Andy Anderson. He developed what was known as the Growth Spiral, which emphasized planning out Sunday School work through the use of a growth plan. The central component of the Growth Spiral was enrolling new members in Sunday school and then continuing to minister to them once enrolled. He said on many occasions, "If you're not enrolled in Sunday School you ain't got no class!" He taught that Sunday School enrollment needs to be "open" or "universal" to use Dr. Ken Hemphill's vernacular. Dr. Anderson said that you should enroll anyone, anywhere, anytime, as long as they agree. Concerning enrollment he had a simple philosophy:

- Start or maintain a roll for each class.
- Keep the roll up to date each week.
- Create a prospect file.
- Engage in a constant search for new prospects.
- Teach and adopt the right approach to enrollment.
- Commit to minister to everyone enrolled.

Finding The Right Combination

How do you define enrollment? Is it a list of people who attend a certain class? Or a list of names by which to check attendance? Or a group of people to whom the leader commits to minister? What is your final answer? Hopefully it is the third choice. Sunday School enrollment is a group of people that God has placed in the care of the Sunday School leader to minister to as well as to teach. I Corinthians 12:18 says: "But now God has set the members, each one of them, in the body just as He pleased." Since God has placed the members in the body of the local church, then He has given you the responsibility to minister to them. It is not only the ones who attend that you are to care for, but for all of those that He has placed in the body.

If you remove names from your enrollment because they do not attend, these people ultimately become lost to the ministry of the church. You who are strong have a responsibility to be patient with and to minister to the weaker members.

The local church needs to have an enrollment policy that reflects this high view of those members that God has placed in the local body. Here are some sample guidelines to consider for setting an enrollment policy in your church:

1. We believe God has placed members in our Body as He has chosen.

2. We will obey the Great Commission in seeking to enroll in Sunday School anyone, anywhere, and any time as long as the person agrees.

3. We will not remove members from the roll unless they join another church, move away from our community, die, or request to have their names removed.

4. We will commit to minister to everyone who is enrolled without regard to his or her frequency of attendance.

There are reasons why churches do not see people enroll in Sunday School. Churches may intentionally or inadvertently erect barriers that prevent people from enrolling. Here are some of the barriers that prevent the growth and the health of the Sunday School:

1. **The "Closed Membership" barrier**: This barrier is one that requires people to be members of the church before they can join the Sunday School. Sunday School needs to be a front door into your church. A person must be a born-again and baptized believer to join the church. However, anyone can join (or be enrolled in) a Sunday School class. A person does not have to be a believer or even a Baptist to join the Sunday School.

> *"Remember, enrollment is a list of people to whom you are committing to minister."*

The evangelistic nature of Sunday School should motivate Sunday School leaders to have the open door policy of enrollment. Enrolling non-members and non-believers will provide the opportunity to minister to believers and non-believers as well as church members and non-members. Ultimately, the class will see people come to know Christ as they pray and minister to everyone on the Sunday School roll.

2. **The "Multiple Sunday Attendance" barrier**: This barrier requires that people attend three or more Sundays before they can enroll. This is a common approach in many churches today. It is totally counter-productive to the growth and health of the Sunday School. A person may join most churches on their first visit if they make a profession of faith or come by letter to unite with the church. Shouldn't it be easier to join the Sunday School than to join the church? Guests should be offered the opportunity to enroll in the Sunday School during their first visit. This has the effect of communicating to guests that they are wanted and needed.

3. **The "In-class Only Enrollment" barrier**: This barrier requires that someone must attend the class before they can be enrolled. An open enrollment approach allows the leader to enroll anyone, anywhere, anytime, as long as they agree. By pre-enrolling people in Sunday School you can prepare in advance for their arrival. Provide them with a nametag and Bible study material that have been prepared before they arrive the first Sunday.

4. **The "Purging the Rolls" barrier**: This is one of the most harmful practices in which Sunday School leaders engage. In an effort to increase their attendance percentages, leaders will purge their rolls of anyone that does not attend regularly. The result of this practice is that contact is lost and ministry ceases to take place. Percentages can be utilized to evaluate some elements of Sunday School health. However, the primary objective of Sunday School is people, not percentages. Purging the rolls to have 100% attendance will only give a false sense of accomplishment. 100% attendance falsely implies that there is no one else to reach. This is never the case!

5. **The "Lack of Motivation" barrier**: What can you do for people that have a lack of motivation to enroll people? This spiritual barrier can only be overcome through prayer, personal training, and encouragement. As leaders you must help people see the big picture of why enrollment is important and model for them the appropriate steps to be taken.

6. **The "Enrollment is Not Important" barrier**: Occasionally you will find people who see Sunday School as only a Bible study. They believe their job is to show up and teach a lesson, giving no regard or attention to ministry and outreach. It will take patience, training, and perhaps the replacement of ineffective leaders to move beyond this barrier.

Breaking Through: How Healthy Sunday Schools Utilize Enrollment

Healthy Sunday Schools tend to be more aggressive in Sunday School enrollment. They recognize that the attendance will not grow if the enrollment remains stable. They understand the thermostat principle as it relates to the attendance in Sunday School. A thermostat is a mechanism utilized to adjust the temperature of a room that is too cool or too warm. The thermostat can be adjusted to raise or lower the temperature of the room. Likewise, the attendance can be lowered or raised with the mechanism of enrollment. Every church that has experienced an increase in enrollment over the past five years has also experienced an increase in Sunday School attendance. Every church that has declined in enrollment over the last five years has also declined in attendance. Those that have maintained the enrollment during that time have a plateaued attendance. You may observe a church that increases enrollment and declines in attendance over the course of a year. However, over a longer period of time the attendance will conform to the direction of the enrollment. Check this for yourself. Compare your current Sunday School enrollment to five years ago. Did your enrollment increase, stabilize, or decrease? Did your attendance follow the same trend?

_____ Enrollment Five Years Ago   _____ Average Attendance Then

_____ Enrollment Today   _____ Average Attendance Now

❏ Increase ❏ Decrease or ❏ Stable?   ❏ Increase ❏ Decrease or ❏ Stable?

The importance of training, contacts, outreach, and relevant teaching cannot be minimized. However, you can do each of these well and you will still not experience sustained growth in attendance without growth in enrollment. Healthy churches understand this fact and utilize enrollment to their advantage. A 2001 study of Georgia's fastest growing Sunday Schools conducted by Sunday School/Open Group Ministries of the Georgia Baptist Convention revealed that these churches overwhelmingly have an aggressive open enrollment approach to Sunday School. Their Sunday School enrollment was, on average, 92% of their resident membership. By contrast, all Georgia Baptist churches combined averaged only 70% of their resident membership on a Sunday School roll.

Consider the following chart outlining the differences between an open enrollment approach as utilized by healthy churches and a closed enrollment approach:

"OPEN ENROLLMENT"	"CLOSED ENROLLMENT"
The roll is a "ministry" list.	The roll is an "attendance" list.
It is easy to get on the roll, but hard to get off of the roll.	It is hard to get on the roll, but easy to get off of the roll.
Leaders are assertive about increasing the enrollment.	Leaders are passive about enrollment.
Anyone may enroll at anytime so long as they agree.	A person may enroll if they show some level of commitment (such as attending three times in a row).
The class is committing to the person enrolled (to minister).	The person enrolled is committing to the class (to attend).
A person remains on the roll as long as the class can provide ministry.	A person remains on the roll until they stop attending regularly.
New Members and Believers are automatically assigned to a class (enrolled).	No one is added until they have attended.
The leaders assign as many of the local (resident) members as possible to classes for ministry.	Members are only on rolls if they attend regularly.
Almost every member receives ministry.	Only faithful attendees receive ministry.

Joining the Sunday School does not equate to joining the church in healthy ministries. Only believers may join the church. However, anyone may join the Sunday School (or be enrolled). By the same token these churches tend to enroll those who join the church into a Bible Study group automatically. There is an assumption that a person that joins the church wants to receive ministry. The ministry arm of these churches is the Sunday School. The research of Georgia's fastest growing Sunday Schools revealed that 84% of them either automatically or strongly encourage enrollment as soon as new members join the church.

How does this aggressive approach impact percentages? The motivation to purge Sunday School rolls is often to increase the percentage of attendance-to-enrollment. In reality this does not greatly affect attendance percentages. The study revealed that the fastest growing Sunday Schools averaged 46% of their enrollment in attendance each Sunday. All churches combined averaged 49% of their enrollment in attendance each Sunday. The churches that tended to be more aggressive in enrollment only

KEY Strategies - FOR HEALTHY SUNDAY SCHOOLS

slightly affected the overall percentage of "enrolled members present." This lower percentage was also a reflection of the more aggressive approach.

How do healthy Sunday School's use percentages of attendance-to-enrollment to strengthen their ministry? While it is true that percentages are not as important as people, they can be a useful tool in evaluation of Sunday School. Effective Sunday School leaders recognize that an average of 40-60% of attendance-to-enrollment is a healthy range. Churches that average more than 60% tend to be those that are weaker in evangelism, outreach, and enrollment practices. Churches that average less than 40% tend to be those that are weaker in ministry, contacts, and care ministry. The key is to maintain a healthy balance between increasing enrollment and maintaining a strong ministry of contacts.

Evaluate your Sunday School by these criteria:
- Do you have an increasing enrollment?
- How does your enrollment compare to your resident membership?
- Is your attendance to enrollment average between 40% and 60%?
- Are new members automatically enrolled?

Do healthy Sunday Schools ever remove people from the roll? Yes, they do. The removal of someone from the roll is done only in the context of the proper definition of enrollment. Enrollment, properly defined, is a list of people to whom the leader commits to minister. Therefore, it is appropriate to remove someone from the roll when they can no longer receive ministry. As previously stated this would include when they die, move, join another church, or request to be removed.

There are still some Sunday Schools, though very few, that do not utilize Sunday School rolls at all. Where do you begin if there has been no focus on Sunday School rolls and/or no system of enrollment?

1. *Determine what type of roll you will use.*
   If you do not have a system in place, you have a couple of options. First, you can purchase enrollment books at your nearest LifeWay Bookstore. These books are great for the smaller Sunday School. They include not only the attendance records, but also space for personal information on each enrollee. Second, computer software programs are available which might make your system more efficient.

These software systems can be customized for your church's needs. There are several vendors available. Talk to your state Sunday School department or customer service through LifeWay resources to find systems they would recommend.

2. *Update rolls for each class.*
   Have a group, an individual, or the teacher make a concerted effort to be sure all information is updated and accurate on everyone that attends the class. Do not drop anyone off the roll at this point. If the roll book is being put together for the first time you will want to get information on anyone who has attended the class in recent months so that they may be enrolled.

   a. *Conduct two registration days.*
      On two consecutive Sundays have everyone present in worship fill out an enrollment card with name, address, phone, age, etc. Be sure this is also done in preschool and other areas where people may not be in the worship service. Ask members and guests to fill the information out completely. Include a place for enrollees to put the name of the class that they are attending if they are active. Collect the cards and be sure they are given to the appropriate classes so that they may begin keeping a roll.

   b. *Conduct a telephone blitz.*
      Follow up the registration days by having teachers call anyone who they are aware was absent during the two-week enrollment promotion period. During the phone blitz, assign a person or group to contact all church members who were also absent during registration. Do not worry if someone gets more than one phone call. It would be better to receive an additional call than to be left out.

   c. *Compile the information and update all rolls.*
      Be sure all cards are placed with the proper class and that all registrants are enrolled. There is no need to ask members of the church if they want to be enrolled. This will be automatic unless they request to be removed. Guests and non-members who were not previously enrolled should be invited to enroll.

3. *Keep accurate weekly records.*
Keep a record in each class of who attends each week. Enroll new and additional members. Keep track of the attendance of individuals. The roll book now becomes a tool. It will allow you to know:

- When individuals miss a Sunday so that you can contact and minister to them;
- Whom you are ministering to;
- Whom to include in fellowship and ministry;
- Whom you can call on;
- How to become more accountable for attendance, growth, ministry, and contacts;
- When new members have enrolled.

Ten Key Ideas That You Can Use

1. *Practice open enrollment.* Enroll people anywhere, any place, and any time as long as they agree. The open enrollment concept is not new. Growing churches have practiced this method of enrollment for decades. Critics of open enrollment say it simply inflates rolls. This is true if you do not follow up with those who have been enrolled. When new enrollees are followed up with a visit, a phone call by class members, and on-going ministry they become legitimate members.

2. *Provide opportunities to enroll during the worship service.* During the morning worship service the majority of churches have a time to welcome guests. Include an enrollment opportunity as part of the guest registration card or place enrollment cards in the pews/chairs and invite guests to enroll from the pews. You will be surprised how many will take advantage of this enrollment opportunity. The cards are then given to the appropriate class to place on their rolls, and then to follow up with a personal in-home visit.

3. *Permit first time guests to Sunday School to enroll.* Each class needs to have enrollment cards or sheets available every Sunday. When guests come, invite them to enroll on their first visit. Explain that you are not asking them to join the church at this time. Let them know that you are the one making the commitment—the

commitment to minister to them. The enrollment card can also serve as a visitor's card for anyone that chooses not to enroll. At the least you will have good information for your follow-up efforts. If they do enroll, you will need to treat them as long-time members from the beginning. Follow-up their enrollment with a personal visit.

4. *Place new church members on a Sunday School roll automatically.* As a policy of the church have all new members automatically enrolled in an age appropriate class or in a new member's or new Christian's class. New members that are not enrolled can easily "slip through the cracks." Through enrolling new members and having them placed into a care group for follow-up you can better assure effective assimilation of new members into the life of the church.

5. *Plan a special enrollment emphasis each year.* Whatever gets focused on gets done. If you will set enrollment goals annually, they will serve as a constant reminder to focus on new people. In addition to weekly enrollment efforts, it is helpful to have a special enrollment campaign each year. This enrollment emphasis can last from a few weeks to a couple of months. The point of this emphasis is to get everyone involved and focused on the main goal of reaching new people. A theme such as "each one reach one" can be a way to promote this effort.

6. *Enroll all resident members.* Make an effort to contact all members of the church that still live in the vicinity and invite them to enroll in a Sunday School class. Explain to them that this is for the purpose of commitment and consistency in ministry on the part of your church. Some of these members may have been removed from the roll because they missed several weeks in a row. A renewed emphasis on prayer and ministry in their lives may renew their interest in attending Bible Study.

7. *Give enrollment cards to outreach teams.* Train those that participate in your visitation ministry to enroll prospects in Sunday School. There are many types of visits that teams will make during the course of a year. Visits are made for ministry, for follow-up of guests to the worship service, for evangelism, to meet new members of the community, etc. Be sure that visitation teams are aware of the opportunity to enroll people in Sunday School during these visits.

8. *Enroll at special events.* Take advantage of opportunities such as fall festivals, children's musicals, drama productions, and other ministry events provided by your church. Invite guests to these events to enroll in a Sunday School group.

9. *Enroll Newborns.* Every child needs to be enrolled in a Sunday School class to provide a foundation of spiritual development from the beginning. Pre-enroll newborns to anticipate their future need for spiritual nurture and ministry. This is also the time to enroll mom and dad in order for them to receive prayer and ministry.

10. *Set enrollment goals.* Many churches set goals for attendance, baptisms, new members, etc. Set a goal that will ensure growth in Sunday School enrollment. It would be unwise for most churches to enroll a massive number of people in the course of a week. Space and leaders to minister to those that enroll must be available. Determine, however, not to allow the enrollment to stay where it is. Set a goal for each class to increase their enrollment by six over the total enrollment of Labor Day weekend. Multiply the number of classes times six to get a total goal for the church. You certainly may set your own goal as God puts it on your heart. But do set a goal. Teachers should constantly be aware of two numbers: their Labor Day enrollment and their current enrollment. This allows them to see where the thermostat has been placed for their class. Likewise, the Sunday School Director, Minister of Education, and Pastor should know these numbers for the total Sunday School.

"Every child needs to be enrolled in a Sunday School class to provide a foundation of spiritual development from the beginning."

KEY #4

CONTACTS ARE MADE WITH CONSISTENCY

Unlocking the Purpose of Contacts

A.V. Washburn wrote a book, Outreach for the Unreached, in which he said, "People are not seeking churches. Churches must seek people. We find nowhere in the New Testament that churches are to teach only those who seek us out. Churches must not wait." In Basic Sunday School Work, Harry Piland said, "Reaching people is a concept originating in the heart of God. It is the purpose that brought Jesus into the world. It is the mark of a spiritually vital church. It is evidence of commitment to Christ. It is our response to a spiritually needy and hungry world." The Great Commission of the Old Testament says, "Assemble the people…so they may hear and learn and fear the Lord your God." (Deuteronomy 31:12). The New Testament is full of verses that compel the church to reach people (Matthew 28:19-20, Acts 1:8, Luke 24:47-48 and John 17:18).

Once the lost have been reached there is no better ministry and assimilation tool than the Sunday School. Remember that the Sunday School enrollment is a group of people whom God has placed in the care of the Sunday School leader to minister to as well as to teach. Contacts are the avenue through which the ministry needs are discovered and responded to. Many leaders mistakenly understand a contact to be simply visitation in the home of a prospect. This is an incomplete perspective that hinders the ministry potential of the Sunday School organization.

Notice that the first word of this key is contacts. A contact is an intentional communication on behalf of the Sunday School class through phone calls, e-mails, visits, post cards, or wayside encounters. The important dynamic of this key is a planned approach (method and timing) to let class members, absentees, and prospects know that they are cared for.

Bo Prosser says, "People go where they know they are cared for and prepared for." Contacts let people know the church and the Sunday School class care for them.

What an appropriate message: "We care about you. We care about you because Jesus does." Whether the person receiving the contact is a prospect or a member, they know they are wanted and that they are cared for.

What happens when a member is absent for several weeks in a row and does not receive a phone call? What happens when a member has a crisis that goes undiscovered and ministry is neglected or overlooked? What happens when a guest visits the class and receives no follow-up communication? What happens when a member begins to serve in a children's class and fails to receive ministry from an adult class? Each of these church members may inadvertently conclude that the class, or even the church, does not care. What a tragedy when this occurs. Everyone has a desire to be cared for. Everyone has needs that can only be met by others. God created man with social needs as well as physical, emotional, mental, and spiritual needs. Everyone wants to have friends and to be a friend to others.

"Contacts are about caring, ministry, and friendship."

The bottom line and the goal are to develop relationships. Contacts provide an avenue and a source of measurement that leaders can use to determine if classes are being intentional in that development.

The ultimate goal of a contact is to communicate caring and to provide ministry. The communication can take many forms:
- "Just wanted to drop off this Sunday School material," you tell the prospect as you give them study materials or curriculum.
- "We missed you Sunday," you say when you see a regular attendee in the grocery store.
- "Do you have any prayer requests that we can be praying for," you say in a phone call to the chronic absentee.
- "The class prayed for you on Sunday," you write in an e-mail to the in-service member.
- "Have a great week," you write on a postcard to an absentee.

A healthy Sunday School contacts individuals consistently based on need. Regular attendees, sporadic attendees, chronic absentees, prospects and in-service members (those individuals who would normally be members of your class but are serving elsewhere in Sunday School) all need contacts throughout the year. They need contacts for various reasons, at various times, in various ways, but all need to be contacted. They all need to know that their group cares about them.

The other important word in this key is consistency. Care cannot be communicated and ministry cannot be provided when individuals go weeks or months without receiving contact. Caring requires consistency. An appropriate attitude and approach toward the class roll and the prospect list is essential to Sunday School health. These lists are composed of people with ministry needs. These are not just lists of people that do attend or that should attend. They are ministry lists that have been providentially placed into the care of the class. It is not possible to genuinely care for people without making consistent contact since this is the key avenue for expressing care and providing ministry. The class must see people as Jesus saw them: "He had compassion on them, because they were harassed and helpless, like a sheep without a shepherd" (Matthew 9:36). When Sunday School leaders and members understand that the enrollment is a ministry list the attitude towards contacts should change from duty to opportunity and from chore to privilege.

Evangelism has been defined as one beggar telling another where to find bread. Likewise, consistently making contacts is like one harassed, helpless sheep telling another where to find the Good Shepherd.

Finding the Right Combination

What does it mean to contact with consistency? What are some general guidelines and goals that let a class or a Sunday School ministry know that consistency is being achieved? The *Sunday School Growth and Evaluation* Plan recommends that the number of weekly contacts should be equal to the number of members enrolled. How many contacts does your class or church average each week? Contacts cannot be measured unless they are reported each week. Healthy Sunday School ministries ask their classes to report the total contacts made each week. Having classes report contacts serves as a tool for accountability, motivation, and measurement. Are your members following up on guests, contacting absentees, and providing ministry to members? Is this an assumption or a reality? Having classes report contacts enables the leadership to have a better understanding of the degree to which ministry and follow-up is or is not taking place. Training leaders and members to understand the purpose for making contacts, methods for contacting, and goals for contacting all serve as a motivation to get as many members as possible involved in this important ministry.

Another goal described in the *Sunday School Growth and Evaluation Plan* is for each class to have the same number of prospects on file as members on the roll. This greatly increases the potential to reach people. One of the most important numbers in Sunday School is the number of prospects a class or department has because it shows the true potential for growth. When you add the number of members on roll with the prospects (which should be the same number) and add in the in-service members there is a sizable number of people to contact. Remember, the goal is to have the number of contacts equal the enrollment. This can be easily achieved when all of these potential contacts are added to the general invitations that the class members extend to friends, family members, and neighbors to attend Sunday School each week.

A healthy Sunday School ministry maintains a balance in providing contacts and ministry to each of these groups. What would happen if all of your emphasis were only on members or only on prospects? What would happen if you contacted some of the people in all three groups but not all of them?

Evaluate the effectiveness of contacts in your church by asking the following questions:
- How many contacts are reported each week?
- To whom are the contacts being made?
- How many people have been enrolled this year?
- How many chronic absentees have been reclaimed this year?
- Did in-service members know about the last fellowship?

Breaking Through: How Healthy Sunday Schools Contact with Consistency
Sunday School is more than a weekly Bible study. An effective Sunday School enables the church to be organized in a way that provides ministry to all of the members. Many needs will not be met if you just assume ministry is being carried out. Organizing for ministry through the Sunday School is a biblical and practical way to minimize the possibility of needs being overlooked. Read Exodus 18 and Acts 6 for examples of the way leaders were encouraged to organize for more effective and efficient ministry.

"Making contacts each week should be a priority because ministry is a priority."

The Sunday School hour should include a time to report the needs and concerns of prospects, absentees and in-service members. Outreach plans and projects will be useless if people are not committed to them and are not ready to conserve the results once people are reached. Committing to make ministry contacts must be included in any comprehensive strategy for developing a healthy Sunday School. A comprehensive strategy will require a two-fold approach to ministry through contacts. The first approach is to train and regularly remind all members of their responsibility for making weekly contacts. The second approach is to establish an organized Care Group Ministry in every adult and youth class. Healthy Sunday School ministries give attention to both approaches.

Train and regularly remind all members of their responsibility for making weekly contacts. Making ministry contact with members and prospects is the responsibility of all Sunday School members. Teachers should be trained to involve as many class members as possible in this crucial task. The teachers should, in turn, train their class members. Class members should become aware of the following as they are trained to participate in the ministry of contacts:

- *Whom* should you contact? Do you know whom you are responsible for contacting? Do you have access to a list of all (active and inactive) class members, in-service members, and prospects? Is the list up to date? Do you regularly invite friends, neighbors, and associates to Sunday School?

- *What* are the needs of the individuals? Do you have access to an attendance summary for each member detailing the number of times they have been to Sunday School? Do you have the information about when the prospect was last contacted, what the results were and what method of contact was used? Are records kept that indicate when and what method was used to contact absentees and active members?

- *What* types of contact methods are available for your use? There are many different types of methods. Each has its own strengths and weaknesses.

1. Home visits:
   Strengths– You can perceive body language and other types of non-verbal communication. You can discover ministry needs that may only be determined

by a personal face-to-face contact. Being on someone else's turf clearly communicates that you think they are worth the effort. An invitation to your home is the most personal contact of all.

Weaknesses– There is a small risk that you may not be well received without an appointment. You can only make limited number of visits in an allotted time. There is a high cost in time and energy.

2. Telephone calls:
   Strengths– Many calls can be made in a short time. A phone call may be appreciated more than a home visit in some communities. There is a low cost in time and energy. You can make calls from many places. A phone call does not require that you dress up. Leaving a message on the answering machine still communicates that you care.

   Weaknesses– You cannot pick up on issues and attitudes that are conveyed through non-verbal communication, interests that are displayed by photographs or awards, etc. These can only be discerned from a personal visit.

3. Cards/Letters:
   Strengths– You can write many in a short time from any place. Everyone eventually gets his or her mail. Care is communicated because of the time expended in writing the note.

   Weaknesses– There is no personal interaction. The amount of communication is minimized. There is a cost involved for postage.

4. E-mail:
   Strengths– There is less formality expected in this form of communication. Delivery is quick and inexpensive. One note can communicate with a large number of people if needed. Response can be made more easily than with traditional mail. This appeals to the technological generation.

   Weaknesses– The note is impersonal if sent to more than one person. There may not be any response or interaction.

5. Wayside encounter:
   Strengths– Personal interaction is involved. There are opportunities in a variety of settings and a variety of times. This is less formal than a home visit.

   Weaknesses– There may be time constraints based on the setting. This does not lend itself to assigned contacts.

   - *Why* are you making the contact? The purpose of the contact will often dictate the method of contact. If it is to share information (upcoming fellowship, class meeting, etc.), a call, card, or e-mail will work. If you are trying to establish a relationship, a visit to their home or an invitation to your home is best. Inviting a family or individual out to dinner can also achieve the same goal. The ultimate purpose is always to discover ministry needs.

   - *When* should you make contact? This addresses the time of day as well as the season of the year. Making home visits during the summer or between Thanksgiving and the New Year is sometimes difficult. There are other times during the year when your community or target group is less likely to be at home (soccer or baseball season, Spring Break). However, everyone does receive their mail, and they do listen to phone messages. There are certain times during the day that a call or a home visit would not be appropriate. Each community and target group has its own standards regarding this. Calls can be made later than visits can be made during the winter months.

People may not volunteer to make contacts if they do not understand the purpose or understand the possible methods of contact. Brainstorm ways to help class members make contacts. Invest time in training class members to be involved. Understand that comfort levels will vary among the members. Find a way for each person to be engaged in contacts at their level of ability and commitment. Ask someone to write post cards or to send some letters for a specific reason. Invite members to come to your home to make phone calls. Ask members to go visiting with you. Challenge them to mentor and involve others in making contacts. Personal attention will take time, but the results are well worth the effort. Be sure that each contact is concluded on a positive note in terms of length (too short is much better than too long) and content. Report to the class any information that might be helpful so that the next person can make a successful contact.

Provide and accept accountability for contacts that are made. There is no way to know how effective the church is being without this information. Provide accountability in a positive way. Notice the subtle difference in these two questions when calling for reports: "John, were you able to contact Joe this week?" or "John, tell me about your contact with Joe this week." The second question focuses on the real purpose for making the contact and assumes involvement in a positive way, focusing on the ministry needs of the person receiving the contact. There will be times when schedules change abruptly and your class member will not be able to make a contact as was intended. There will be times when the person being contacted will not be available. Allow your class member to be honest and simply report this. Most people will respond positively when the climate permits this. A positive and encouraging environment is essential to motivating class members to participate.

Be sure to provide to the class leadership information that is current about the person that is contacted. This also includes ministry needs that are discovered so long as confidentiality is not breached. It is imperative that the class has up-to-date information on prospects and members. Also make sure the church office or other appropriate persons receive information from contacts. Many pastors have been embarrassed because a person was admitted and released from the hospital without their knowledge. Communicate ministry needs to the appropriate persons as soon as possible. The same would be true if you discover that a person has moved or changed church membership. Assist the church by communicating this information. It has been said that an army travels on its stomach. An army can go no farther than its supply lines can support. The contacting "army" travels on current, useful information. Help your church avoid operating on invalid or outdated information by making contacts on behalf of your class each week.

Establish an organized Care Group Ministry in every adult and youth class.
Remember that enrollment is a group of people to whom the leader commits to minister. The teacher of the class commits to provide leadership and ministry to the class as well as to teach a weekly Bible study. This can be a great challenge when enrollment is fifteen, twenty, twenty-five, or even higher. How can the teacher maintain consistent contact with each member in order to provide ministry? If consistent contact is not made there will be absentees that go unnoticed, ministry needs that go unmet, and regular members that may not feel appreciated. Making consistent ministry contacts is essential. However, the teacher cannot do this alone.

Each youth and adult class should organize care groups to insure that ministry contacts are made on a regular basis. This is consistent with the principles for sharing the load of ministry found in Exodus 18 and Acts 6.

The teacher may choose to enlist a Care Group Coordinator. This person would be responsible for enlisting Care Group Leaders. The Care Group Coordinator's responsibilities are to:

1. Enlist one Care Group Leader from the class for each four to seven individuals or couples enrolled in the class.

2. Provide the Care Group Leader with as much information as possible on the members assigned to their care.

3. Call every Care Group Leader on Thursday night to receive a report on contacts made, to ask for any prayer requests that they might have, and/or to remind them to contact each person on their ministry list.

4. Report ministry concerns to the teacher or pastor as warranted.

5. Train Care Group Leaders to fulfill their ministry responsibilities.

6. Re-organize Care Groups (every four to six months) by enlisting additional leaders and making reassignments as needed in order to maintain manageable ministry lists.

The care group leader's responsibilities are to:

1. Within one week of assignment, call each person assigned to their group. Get to know them personally. Write down biographical information including the names and birth dates of all family members, mailing address, e-mail address, wedding anniversary, special interests, information on church involvement, and any other information that would be helpful in providing ministry.

2. Visit with each assigned person in their home, have them in your home, or go out to dinner with them within four weeks of the assignment.

3. Call each member of the care group each Monday or Tuesday night (this should be no more than four to seven calls if organized properly). Be sure to ask, "Do you have any prayer requests for this week?" This question will help to determine ministry needs. The same question is appropriate whether they attend each week, occasionally, or never. Pray for any needs discovered and assist in meeting them when and if possible. Maintain confidentiality when appropriate.

4. Report ministry concerns to the Care Group Coordinator, teacher, or pastor as warranted.

5. Acknowledge birthdays, anniversaries, special accomplishments, etc. of family members of the individuals or couples assigned.

6. Develop a relationship with those assigned to the greatest degree possible in order to provide encouragement and ministry.

Have you ever known someone that was in the hospital that did not receive a visit from the pastor? Almost every pastor has experienced the horror of discovering that someone was admitted and released from the hospital without his knowledge. The issue was not a lack of concern on his part; the problem was that no one communicated the need with him. This will not happen if the Sunday School class is functioning properly. What if every member or family received a call from someone in your church every week? Organizing care groups can make this possibility a reality.

Oak Hill Baptist Church in Griffin, Georgia was identified as the church with the fastest growing Sunday School in Georgia in 2001. The church grew from 76 to 1,128 in average attendance in eight years. The *Christian Index* featured the church in an article in August of 2001. The article read in part:

> "Lots of churches have high expectations, but not all of them inspect it. We have a teacher covenant, and we're highly accountable. Among other things, teachers are expected to attend all services, to tithe, and to call every one of their class members every week. Calling is how we find out what is going on in the life of the people. Sometimes the teacher calls, sometimes they have callers assigned to call. But everyone gets a call every week. This method helps keep the frustration level down."

Ten Key Ideas That You Can Use

1. *Ask all Adult classes to enlist a Care Group Coordinator.* The Care Group Coordinator is responsible for enlisting care group leaders, organizing care groups, and contacting all care group leaders each week. This person should continually re-organize and re-evaluate the care group structure in order to insure contact with each family in the church each week.

2. *Expect all classes to organize into care groups.* The teacher would have difficulty making fifteen to forty contacts each week. Organizing into Care Groups allows each Care Group Leader to make only four to five calls each week. This is the most logical way to insure that every family in the church receives contact and ministry each week. Every member should be called every week.

3. *Have each class report total contacts made each week.* Reporting contacts provides a source of measurement for evaluation and improvement. Everyone is responsible for assisting with contacts. The teacher, class coordinator, or care group coordinator should take some time each Sunday to ask members to report the total contacts they made during the last week. This can be done by having class members hold up their fingers to correspond to the number of contacts made. A chart could be formed and passed around that would allow the members to record the number of contacts made that week. Reporting contacts serves as motivation and a reminder to the members. It insures a level of accountability.

4. *Report contacts in the same way that attendance is reported.* Emphasize the importance of contacts by publishing, posting, and reporting contacts in any and all venues where attendance is reported. This will serve as a reminder to all who see the reported information that contacts are essential to the health of the Sunday School ministry.

5. *Make Saturday night calls.* Call all of your members and prospects on Saturday night. Tell them that you look forward to seeing them in Sunday School tomorrow. Do this a few times and watch attendance climb.

6. *Hold a contact rally.* After the morning worship service, invite members to stay and eat lunch in preparation for going out to make contacts. Assign one or two

classes to prepare and serve the meal. Use disposable items so no one is "stuck" with clean up. This type of gathering is weatherproof and can involve a great number of people. Personal enlistment is key to a good turnout. In addition, it is imperative that there be an ample number of contacts to be made. Make sure all prospect cards are up to date. Have available all the necessary information on absentees. Be sure to have all the needed supplies on hand. Some members may choose to stay at the church and write cards or make phone calls, while others may choose to make home visits. Some teams may decide to go out and do a prospect search. Have people sign out and set up a time for everyone to return for a celebration time. Celebrate with each team as they report how they saw God work as they made contacts.

7. *Prayer call.* The class Prayer Leader begins this "chain" by calling all of the Care Group Leaders. They call their members and simply ask each person if they have any prayer requests that need to be taken to the class the next Sunday. The Care Group Leaders then call the class Prayer Leader back with all of the requests. The class Prayer Leader types them up, makes copies, and distributes these requests for the prayer time on Sunday.

8. *Hot and Spicy.* Stop by the home of a first time guest just long enough to leave a bag of chips and jar of salsa.

9. *PIE– "People Involved in Evangelism."* Take a pie to a prospect or new move-in. Tell them you will come back later to pick up the dish. Talk with them about Sunday School at the second visit.

10. *Furniture Talks.* Have enough chairs in your room for both enrollees and prospects. Write the name, phone number and address of each person– prospect and enrollee– on a 3x5 card. Place a card in each chair. As people come to class, have them pick up their card. Make contact assignments for those cards that are remaining. Do this for an entire month. It shows very obviously the potential of the class.

KEY #5

LEADERS ARE TRAINED FOR EFFECTIVENESS

Unlocking The Purpose of Training Leaders

"Sunday School Leader Training, in my estimation, is the most important meeting in the church. If you use this meeting correctly, it will revolutionize the church. If you use this meeting incorrectly, you will continue to limp along without sufficient quantity, quality, or power."

–Andy Anderson

Over 94% of Southern Baptist churches in Georgia report that they have weekly Sunday School or Bible study groups. They all meet at about the same time, are generally organized in the same way, have a teacher leading a Bible study, and gather on a weekly basis. You would think that they would be getting similar results since they are all doing basically the same thing. Yet, this is not the case. Approximately one-third of these Sunday Schools are reaching new people and growing. In addition to the Bible study there is a sense of excitement, people are coming to know Christ, and the classes have developed into ministry centers for their members. Why are one-third of the churches getting good results while the others are not? One of the crucial differences is related to training.

July has arrived in the local church and the nominating committee has begun its work. Teachers are being enlisted for the new Sunday School year. Over half of the teachers from the previous year have agreed to stay. Many have taught the same class for several years. The next wave of enlistment comes as a couple of members feel compelled to serve in whatever way they can to best help their church. They do not have any experience or training, but they do have a deep commitment to the Lord. Enlisting for the last few positions is quite a challenge. Announcements are made from the pulpit with the call becoming more desperate by the week. The next wave of volunteers that agree to serve are those that propose, "If no one else will do it, I will." They have the willingness, despite any lack of passion or training. Members who have been begged to help "lest the middle school boys have no leader at all" fill those final spots. The teachers are provided with curriculum and launch into the year with a commitment to teach each week. Some of the teachers are skilled in their presentations while the others simply do the best they can.

Their entire focus each week is on lesson preparation and presentation. In some cases the preparation is an afterthought. In others, the presentation could be marketed as a sedative. The teacher does not involve anyone other than a class secretary to turn in a report each week. No one new is enrolled for several months. In addition, several people are removed from the roll because of their lack of attendance. There are no sustained attempts at outreach, and the class does not have the privilege of seeing anyone come to know Christ. The teacher's sole purpose is to teach a lesson each week. Hopefully, this does not sound like a description of your situation. It is, however, an apt description of a church that does not provide training for Sunday School leaders.

Training leaders to be effective is vital to the health of the Sunday School. Training is a systematic approach for conveying necessary skills to leaders that permit them to effectively carry out the ministry to which God has called them. Look at what Paul said to Timothy in II Timothy 1:3-5:

> *I thank God, whom I serve with a clear conscience the way my forefathers did, as I constantly remember you in my prayers night and day, longing to see you, even as I recall your tears, so that I may be filled with joy. For I am mindful of the sincere faith within you, which first dwelt in your grandmother Lois, and your mother Eunice, and I am sure that it is in you as well.*

Paul points out three things that were true of Timothy. Timothy had been <u>helpful</u> to Paul. Timothy was his son in the faith and in ministry. Paul constantly remembered Timothy and prayed for him out of gratitude for their relationship. Timothy had a good <u>heart</u>. Paul remembered Timothy's tears and the compassionate heart that is described in Acts and the epistles of Paul. Timothy had a strong heritage. Paul reminded him that his faith was passed down from faithful family members. Timothy had a helpful spirit, a good heart, and a strong <u>heritage</u>. Yet, this was not enough. Paul then follows up in II Timothy 1:6 by reminding him: "Therefore I remind you to kindle afresh [stir up] the gift of God which is in you through the laying on of my hands."

Timothy could not rely on his good qualities alone to make him the leader that he needed to be. Paul challenged him to "kindle afresh" his God given gifts. This is an ongoing process. The same could be said of Sunday School leaders in churches today. They generally have helpful spirits, good hearts, and often a strong heritage. Their love of God, concern for their church, and commitment to God is not necessarily at issue. However, they can have these good qualities, as Timothy did, and still provide weak leadership. In addition to these qualities they need to "kindle afresh" the gift that is within them.

> *"You cannot simply enlist a leader, give them curriculum, pat them on the back, and expect them to be effective."*

You must purposefully help them to grow in their skills as a leader if they are to be effective. How are they to know the keys to a healthy Sunday School ministry unless they are communicated and then applied?

Who is responsible for training Sunday School leaders? Ephesians 4:11-12 says, "And He gave some as apostles, and some as prophets, and some as evangelists, and some as pastors and teachers, for the equipping of the saints for the work of service to the building up of the body of Christ (emphasis added)." The responsibility for equipping leaders begins with the Pastor and the staff. This is one of the key reasons God provided the church with these leaders. This may or may not mean that the Pastor leads the actual equipping sessions. It does mean that he initiates and provides equipping in order that the body of Christ will be strengthened. Equipping is the responsibility of the Pastor.

Equipping is also the responsibility of the Minister of Education. Likewise, equipping is the responsibility of the Minister to Students, Children, or Preschool. No Pastor or staff member should be waiting on someone else to equip or provide training for their leaders. Equipping is also the responsibility of the Sunday School Director. The Director's responsibility does not end with counting the number of people present on Sunday morning. The Sunday School Director is a leader engaged in strengthening the Sunday School by all means including training of the Sunday School leadership team.

One further point must be emphasized in regard to the issue of who is responsible. Even if a Pastor, staff member, or Sunday School Director neglects this biblical responsibility, it does not absolve the Sunday School leader or teacher of their

responsibility to rekindle (stir up) the gift of God that is in them.
Does it really matter if Sunday School leaders receive training? What difference does it make if a church has trained or untrained Sunday School leaders? Consider what happens when the Sunday School leaders are trained:

1. *The leaders are less likely to burn out:* There is no joy in struggling through a ministry. Doing something well and seeing results serves as added motivation. Training allows the leader to improve his or her skills, set appropriate priorities, understand the purpose of his or her ministry, and to make wise and efficient use of time and resources.

2. *The leaders will be more effective:* Would you prefer to visit a trained doctor or an untrained doctor? Would you prefer that your first grade child have a trained or an untrained schoolteacher? The potential illustrations are endless. Would you prefer for your preschool child or grandchild to be led by a trained or an untrained preschool leader? You might insist that you know preschool leaders that love children and do a good job that are not trained. There is no question that they have a good heart. However, there is more to preschool Sunday School than caring for the toddlers for an hour. It is also an instructional time. Do the teachers have the skills to provide care, safety, instruction, and an inviting environment? A trained leader, in any age group, is going to have a distinct advantage over an untrained leader.

3. *The leaders will receive a better response from the class members:* It has been said that the main reason that people do not go to Sunday School is because they have been. Sadly, there are classes that are lifeless, cold, and academic. This is not the way that Sunday School is supposed to be. A trained leader will think about their leadership, will grow in their leadership, and will grow in their communication skills. There are some teachers that are gifted communicators; some have to learn good communication. Today's culture, more than ever, requires a skilled communicator. Do the leaders know about learning styles and teaching methods? Do they know how to organize the class, how to develop new leaders, and how to reach the lost through the Sunday School ministry? Any leader with a willing heart can be trained to do these things and will ultimately receive a greater response from those who follow.

4. *The leaders will raise up more leaders:* A trained teacher will understand that he or she cannot accomplish the purpose of Sunday School alone. They will begin to organize the class and bring others alongside to accomplish the ministry. They will develop a team committed to reaching out and ministering rather than a group interested only in exercising a "gift" of pew or chair sitting while watching the teacher doing all of the ministering.

5. *The enlistment process will be enhanced:* Most churches that have an enlistment problem have a training problem. The number of available leaders will grow as trained Sunday School leaders effectively organize the ministries of their class and involve more of the members. This principle is true in relation to the quality of prospective leaders as well as the quantity. It does not happen overnight. Churches that effectively equip have much less of a strain at enlistment time than those that do not train leaders.

6. *The leaders will reach and minister to more people:* The trained leader will be able to care for more people and see more people come to Christ through the ministry of the class because he or she will be skilled in motivating and organizing the class. The focus will extend beyond teaching as the leaders understand the true purpose of Sunday School.

Finding The Right Combination

"The task of the Sunday School is too vital to leave training to chance. The church must have a strategy for ongoing training of Sunday School leadership, or the leadership pool will continue to shrink. People are more likely to serve if they know that the church will provide them the resources and necessary training. Jesus instructed His disciples before He sent them out into ministry (Matt. 10:5)."

-Ken Hemphill

It is undeniable that Pastors, staff, and Sunday School Directors have a responsibility to equip the Sunday School leaders. How should a church evaluate themselves in this key area? The first question is simple: Does the church have a systematic approach for training Sunday School leaders? Are the leaders expected to receive training and is it provided on a regular basis? A study of Georgia's fifty fastest growing Sunday Schools was conducted by Sunday School/Open Group Ministries of the Georgia Baptist Convention in 2001. One of the outstanding findings related to the training of leaders. All but one of the churches, or 98%, reported that they have a systematic approach to leader training. Could it be that the reason they are among the fastest growing Sunday Schools is because they have trained and skilled leaders? That is at least a portion of the explanation.

These churches were all sizes and in all types of communities and settings. The fact that they train their leaders was one of the most overwhelming common practices related to Sunday School. 84% of these churches provided training on a monthly or weekly basis. Another 11% met at least quarterly. A total of 95% met at least quarterly. Of these churches, 92% provided training opportunities in addition to the regular weekly, monthly, or quarterly training. The remaining churches provided training in a variety of other ways (see samples in Ten Key Ideas section). The first key to finding the right combination is to institute a system of training.

The second question a church should ask is: How many of the leaders participate in the training opportunities? The training will be of no effect unless the leaders are availing themselves of the training. It is essential that the Sunday School teachers receive training. However, effective churches move beyond the teachers and provide training for all Sunday School leaders. Sunday School leaders include Department Directors, Class Secretaries, Prayer Coordinators, Outreach Leaders, Class Coordinators, Care Group Coordinators, Care Group Leaders, Apprentice Teachers, and as many other leaders as have specific responsibilities with the Sunday School. The ultimate goal is to seek an average participation of 75% of all Sunday School leaders in each regular (weekly, monthly, or quarterly) training session. It is important to start where you are. Your goal may begin with expecting 75% of the teachers to participate in each session. However, it is vital that you slowly raise the standard as time goes by. If you aim low you will receive low results.

What if you're experiencing low participation? Some Pastors, Ministers of Education, staff members, and/or Sunday School directors inadvertently hinder participation. The following are ways that leaders can hamper participation in training:

1. *Provide inadequate training:* Leaders can joke that the reason that some people do not go to Sunday School is because they have been, but there is an element of truth to this statement. Sadly, staff members themselves are the most likely to

use this reasoning to avoid training. Staff members should be the most skilled communicators in the church with a readiness to equip others. Perhaps the following question should be posed: Why do Sunday School leaders not want to attend training sessions? Could it be because they have been? You cannot expect teachers to prepare an outstanding lesson, arrive early to the class, provide a healthy environment, and deliver a dynamic lesson while the church hosts or provides training sessions that are ill prepared, irrelevant, or potentially mistaken for funeral services.

2. *Have the attitude that "my leaders won't participate":* This is a tragic statement when spoken by a Pastor or staff member. John Maxwell, of Injoy Ministries, has always asserted, "Leadership is influence." He says, "He who thinks he leadeth and has no one following is only taking a walk." Regardless of the title that one possesses there is a forfeiture of leadership that occurs once this negative attitude prevails in the minds of the other leaders. Why are there some churches where the Sunday School leadership gladly and willingly participate in training? They participate because of the influence and leadership of those given responsibility for the Sunday School as well as because of the quality of the training provided.

3. *Have low expectations:* Thom Rainer, President of LifeWay Christian Resources, has done extensive research in the area of church health and church growth. His works include: *Effective Evangelistic Churches, High Expectations*, and *Surprising Insights from the Unchurched*. He is a tremendous advocate of the importance of the role of Sunday School in healthy churches. He consistently concludes in his research that churches that have higher levels of expectations of leaders are more effective in evangelism and assimilation. Instituting commitments and covenants for your leaders can be a painful process. The introduction of expectations often brings a mild storm and the potential loss of some leaders. However, churches that are willing to weather this storm find that the quality of leadership improves dramatically and the higher level of expectations bring about greater results. Why would you want a leader that does not feel that they need any level of training? No leader serves without room for growth and improvement.

4. *Expect all to participate in every session and whine about those that do not:* "I would go to the Sunday School conference, but most of my leaders cannot go." Who says they all have to go? Ideally, everyone would participate in everything that is offered. However, this is not an ideal world. Expect everyone to participate

in training, but understand that everyone cannot or will not participate in some training activities. Expend your energy rejoicing over those that do participate instead of complaining about those that do not. What do you do if only three of your leaders agree to go to the Sunday School conference that you have promoted? Go and have a great time! What if you provide a training session and less than half of the leaders attend? Lead with enthusiasm and give it your best! The quality of those leaders that do participate will increase as the months go by. Recognize and celebrate those leaders that are growing in their skills. Participation in training will eventually become the norm if you stay on course.

5. *Base attitudes about training on a bad experience:* Some leaders who have attended training sessions in the past on a local, associational, or state level may not have had a pleasant experience. There is no reason or excuse for this, but a single bad experience should not influence future decisions. I was once taken to a Chinese restaurant as a child. My parents ordered for me since I was not familiar with the menu. I did not like the taste of the food at all. Following this experience, I flinched at any invitation to go to a Chinese restaurant. Fifteen years later I was prodded into going with a fellow staff member. He ordered a completely different dish than what my parents had ordered. I loved it and realized that there was more to Chinese food than what I had experienced as a child. Now I eat Chinese food two or three times a month. One or two bad experiences at a conference or in training do not mean that every opportunity will be the same. Be sure that when the training is in your charge that you do not leave a bad taste in anyone's mouth because you are ill prepared or irrelevant.

The third question that should be asked to evaluate training is: What variety of training is being offered? What level of participation should be expected?

> *"Remember, the goal in an effective church is to average 75% of leaders present in regular, ongoing training (weekly or monthly)."*

There are a variety of other opportunities that leaders can take advantage of in order to grow in their skills. These include, but are not limited to, national, state, regional, and associational Sunday School training events. These may be directly or indirectly related to Sunday School. These could also include opportunities at the church that are in addition to the regular training. These could include, but are not limited to, a launch event in August, new leader orientation, a leader appreciation banquet, a regional event hosted by the church, a leader retreat, etc. The goal for participation is to get each leader, 100%, to participate in one or more of these type of training opportunities in the course of the year (See Ten Key Ideas at conclusion of this section for other possibilities).

The fourth question for evaluating leadership training is: How many leaders does the church have and need in order to be effective? Obviously, three leaders in a class can accomplish more than one. Six can accomplish more than three. A class is going to be healthier and more effective as more leaders are identified. Remember, teachers are not the only leaders in Sunday School. Leaders in Sunday School include Directors, Class Secretaries, Class Coordinators, Outreach Coordinators, Prayer Coordinators, Apprentice Teachers, Care Group Coordinators, Care Group Leaders, and any other person that has specific assignments and responsibilities for leadership in the Sunday School. A teacher or Class Coordinator should enlist as many people within the class as possible to serve on a leadership team. Effective churches move beyond the enlistment of the teacher and account for and train as many leaders as possible. The goal is to have one leader identified for every five people enrolled in Sunday School. For example: a church that has an enrollment of 140 with an average attendance of 60. The church has seven classes. If the church emphasizes only the seven teachers there is a ratio of one leader for every twenty enrolled. This church is unlikely to experience growth in the coming year. This church should set a goal of identifying and training twenty-eight leaders to attain the ratio of 1:5. If this has not been the practice, it may take a few weeks following the beginning of the new Sunday School year for the teachers to organize the class and enlist leaders within the class. In addition, the younger aged classes will need the smallest ratios. (Refer back to Key #2 for recommended ratios.)

Breaking Through: How Healthy Sunday Schools Utilize Training

A key to regular attendance at the meeting is that you recruit leaders with the understanding that attendance is expected. You will find that many persons actually respond positively to the greater level of demand. Most churches would not consider having a choir that did not gather for rehearsal. They would be ill prepared to lead in worship. In similar fashion, it is difficult to think that we would entrust the teaching of God's Word to persons who did not have the commitment to meet for planning and prayer.

–Ken Hemphill

Effective Sunday Schools have an expectation that all leaders participate in training. The preceding sections laid out the case for why training should be expected and the advantages of equipping the Sunday School leadership. The issue of how to increase participation is addressed throughout this chapter. What do you do if this is a new concept to your church? How do you introduce and implement these expectations if the staff has not provided training and/or if teachers have been enlisted without written standards in the past? Begin by enlisting a team to develop written ministry descriptions for key leaders. Include training expectations in the descriptions. Identify minimal expectations with a list of five or six points at the most. These can be expanded in later years as expectations are raised. Once completed, present these to the leaders as *general guidelines*. The leaders do not need to sign these at this point. Give these to leaders upon enlistment the next time your Sunday School year begins. The following year transition the heading for the *general guidelines* to leadership commitment. The leaders make a verbal commitment to serve by these standards as they are enlisted. The final phase is to transition from leadership commitment to leadership covenants where leaders sign a covenant to serve by the written standards. At this point the leaders are absolutely committed to participate in the equipping plan as proposed in the covenant.

The level of comfort varies from church to church in relation to how far to carry the implementation of commitments and covenants. Having no written guidelines or descriptions is a recipe for low expectations and low results. Implement the *general guidelines* at a minimum. According to a 2001 study of Georgia's fastest growing Sunday Schools, conducted by the Sunday School/Open Group Ministries of the Georgia Baptist Convention, 78% of these churches utilize *leadership commitments* or *leadership covenants*. 20% provide *general guidelines* for their leaders. Only one of the churches did not address expectations in any formal or informal manner. This is overwhelming evidence that higher expectations can be successfully implemented and that they are critical to the effectiveness and health of Sunday School.

Effective Sunday Schools evaluate their current approaches to training in order to plan and improve. Use these questions, based on the previous section, as a starting point for evaluation:

1. Does the church have a systematic approach for training Sunday School leaders? Has the quality of the training improved over previous years?

2. How many leaders, not just teachers, are participating in training opportunities?

3. What variety of training is being offered, and what level of participation is expected?

4. How many Sunday School leaders can be identified? What is the ratio of leaders to enrollment?

Effective Sunday Schools establish measurements and goals to enhance training and participation. The leader of the Sunday School (Pastor, Minister of Education, or Sunday School Director) should maintain the following records related to training issues and set goals to improve and maintain minimum standards in subsequent years:

1. Average attendance present at regular (weekly or monthly) training sessions. The goal is to average 75% of all leaders in attendance.

2. The number of leaders that have participated in an additional training opportunity beyond regular (weekly or monthly) training in the course of the year. The goal is to have 100% of leaders participate in an "extra mile" opportunity.

3. The number of identifiable Sunday School leaders and the ratio of leaders to enrollment. The goal is to move toward, and then maintain, a ratio of one leader to every five enrolled in Sunday School.

Effective Sunday Schools provide and host regular (monthly or weekly) leadership training sessions that are worthy of attendance by the leaders. These training sessions should be well prepared and marked by extra touches that encourage and reward the participation of the Sunday School leaders. These extra touches relate to the quality of the environment in which the training is to occur:

1. Provide childcare to encourage and assist with the participation of leaders with small children.

2. Provide a meal or a snack to assist those that may not have enjoyed a meal in recent hours. This also encourages fellowship.

3. Prepare the room well in advance. Prior to the arrival of the leaders, chairs, tables, supplies, refreshments, audio/video equipment, sound systems and all elements related to the environment should be in place. The leaders arrive to the prepared environment with music playing and light snacks available.

4. The training should begin and end on time. Key leaders for the meeting have prepared and arrived early (just as teachers are instructed to do for Sunday School), and the attendees are assured that the time will be used wisely with no doubt that it will conclude at the stated time.

5. The time should not be crowded with announcements. Anything that can be read should be written down. Only one or two key announcements should be made verbally during the training.

6. The training should include a time of inspiration. Special music, testimonies, prayer, worship, praise reports, special recognitions, and/or some other inspirational element should be used to set the tone for the training time.

7. Instruction should always be relevant and worthy of the time being spent.

8. The person responsible should be a person that refuses to host a boring training session.

9. Time should be balanced well between inspiration, instruction, and planning. The planning generally should take place in departmental groupings during the last one-third to one-quarter of the time available.

Ten Key Ideas That You Can Use

"An untrained Soldier is nothing more than a target for the enemy!"

–Andy Anderson

1. *Provide a reasonable schedule based on where you are now.* Perhaps your church has not provided regular, ongoing training in the past. Scheduling a weekly leadership training time and instituting teacher covenants may be too great a leap to make at one time. The goal should be to provide quality, regular, ongoing training. This

will ultimately mean that leaders will be making a greater commitment and that training will be held at least monthly. Start where you are. Those churches that have provided no training might begin with quarterly training, participation in a state or associational conference, and general guidelines that are developed for leaders. The key is to evaluate where you are and to raise the bar each year. There will be a point where the quantity of training will level out at a maximum that can be expected of volunteers. However, the quality of training can be improved each and every year.

2. *Send a representative group to all associational and state training opportunities.* This is not to suggest that everyone should not be invited or encouraged to attend any and all training opportunities. Ideally, all of your leaders would take advantage of quality training. Do not discount the value of an opportunity simply because a large percentage of your leaders cannot participate. Send a single representative or representative group from each division to attend and report back to all other leaders. This will allow your leaders to gain the benefit of new ideas and resources that are available to strengthen them in their leadership roles.

3. *Provide opportunities for your leaders to receive training in non-traditional ways.* Each leader should be encouraged to grow in their skills by taking advantage of regularly scheduled training as well as taking some personal initiative. Tapes, books, DVD's, and/or Internet resources can be accessed at a time convenient to the individual. Purchase and provide resources that leaders can checkout and return. CD's can be listened to driving to and from work. DVD's can be viewed on a schedule chosen by the individual leader.

Tim Smith, a Sunday School/Open Group Ministries Consultant with the Georgia Baptist Convention, regularly adopts churches for long term mentoring. He enhances the training of the leaders by having the church purchase one of four recommended books for each leader. The leaders are then grouped in teams of four. Each team member's name is written in the front of each book. Each person is challenged to read the first book during the month before passing it along to another team member whose name is listed at the front of the book. The leaders read four books in the course of four months that give them the knowledge and skills they need to be more effective leaders. Remember, healthy Sunday Schools encourage their leaders to involve themselves in something each year above and beyond regularly scheduled training. A personally initiated skill-building activity such as one of those listed here could be utilized as well as could an invitation to participate in an associational, state, or national training event.

4. *Record all leadership training sessions.* The goal is to average 75% participation in regular (monthly or weekly) training opportunities. This goal assumes that everyone cannot participate in every training session. Always audiotape training sessions provided by your church. Make copies of the CD's or tapes to give to all leaders that could not attend. This will allow the leaders that were absent to receive the information, training, and encouragement that they missed. This would not serve as a substitute for their regular participation. Taking advantage of this method or using other emerging technologies that would serve the same purpose will maximize training.

5. *Provide leadership diplomas to recognize and reward participation in training.* At the conclusion of each year, publicly recognize all leaders that participate in the minimum amount of training that is recommended or to which they committed. Give greater recognition to those that go beyond the minimum expectations in their training. The minimum can be the number of hours of training described in the Sunday School leaders general guidelines or leadership commitments. Another option is to allow each individual leader to set their personalized level (number of hours) of training as part of the enlistment and commitment process. Providing leadership diplomas reinforces the value of training and allows the church to affirm and express appreciation for the development of the leader's skills.

6. *Familiarize your leaders with Internet resources.* Supplemental training, resources, and ideas are readily available now via the Internet. Go to ssog.gabaptist.org to access the website of Sunday School/Open Group Ministries of the Georgia Baptist Convention to find a variety of resources as well as links to other sites that supplement the training you provide. This website is available to your teachers 24/7 at their convenience.

7. *Begin the year with a launch event.* Take advantage of the enthusiasm that exists at the beginning of each Sunday School year by hosting a launch event. This is both a training session and an orientation to get your leaders prepared for the new Sunday School year. This session should be more intense and in-depth than

the regular leadership meeting. Schedule a weeknight or Sunday evening for a two to three hour training session. This is a great opportunity to address organizational issues, review general guidelines or leadership commitments, distribute literature, and provide motivation for the upcoming year. You can invite a guest speaker to provide a fresh voice or allow key leaders within the church to lead the training. LifeWay Christian Resources also has a Launch Kit that is available for purchase each summer.

8. *Host an annual Sunday School leader appreciation banquet.* This annual banquet can also serve as a training opportunity. February is a great month to host the banquet. The leaders are half way through the Sunday School year at this point. The banquet serves as a great time of fellowship and an expression of appreciation. In addition, a church leader or guest speaker can re-emphasize key points to the participating leaders as they share an inspirational message as part of the evening's schedule.

9. *Host a leadership retreat.* Arrange for as many leaders as possible to spend a Friday night and Saturday morning on location or off location for a time of intensive training and motivation. Bring in skilled leaders to equip your teachers to be the best that they can be.

10. *Provide a twelve-month calendar of training opportunities at the beginning of the Sunday School year.* Participation can be strengthened if the leaders know in advance what training opportunities are available and when they will occur. You cannot announce a training event two weeks ahead of time and expect strong attendance. Before the beginning of the Sunday School year, plan the schedule of regular (monthly or weekly) training times, a launch event, an appreciation banquet, state and associational training events, and non-traditional alternatives. This can be placed in the leader's hands as soon as they are enlisted. They can begin to place these opportunities on their calendars and plan to participate well in advance. Print and provide the twelve-month calendars during enlistment and again as the new Sunday School year begins.

KEY Strategies - FOR HEALTHY SUNDAY SCHOOLS

KEY #6

TEACHING THAT IS RELEVANT TO THE AUDIENCE

Unlocking The Purpose of Teaching that is Relevant to the Audience

Have you ever taken a really long road trip? When I was 12 years old I spent my summer vacation riding with members of my family from Georgia all the way up the east coast to Newfoundland, Canada. It was an amazing trip. We stopped in every state and province to experience some local culture. We ate all different styles of food. We stayed in hotels, campgrounds, and even slept in our van one night. I still have pictures from that trip. But what amazes me is that when I think back on this trip, it is not the culture, the food or the places we stayed that I remember; it is the van ride with my family that I remember most. It was the shared experiences that I had with my family in that van that will stay with me for a lifetime.

As I think back on that trip, it helps me to understand how important the Sunday School classroom experience really is. You see, we can know the purpose of Sunday School, have a great organization and plenty of space, but if our teaching and classroom experience isn't what it should be, then Sunday School could still be a disaster.

> *"Your Sunday School class should not be defined simply by the number of people you have enrolled or the room in which you meet."*

Your class should be defined by the life transformation that is taking place through relevant teaching. Before we look at what relevant teaching is, it might help to take a look at some ineffective teaching methods.

- **Teaching without preparation–** The most important time for a teacher is not the minutes that he will stand in front of their class to teach, but the hours that go into the preparation of the lesson. An unprepared teacher is an ineffective teacher.

- **Teaching without application–** Some teachers think their task is to simply impart Biblical knowledge to their learners. Instead teachers should look for opportunities to engage their classes in some kind of specific response to the content. Learners need to handle the material in some way to make the content personal.

- **Teaching without passion**– Teaching just to cover the material lacks passion and excitement. If your goal is to simply get through the class session or to cover this section, then you are probably missing passion. Passion is communicated when we have allowed the Scriptures that we are teaching to penetrate our own hearts and minds.

- **Teaching without people in mind**– Hopefully when you teach there are actually people there that are listening and ready to learn. If not, then you've got problems bigger than we can handle in this book. Your teaching should target the individuals in your class. Visualize each learner in your class and decide which parts of the content apply to that learner. Then develop a lesson plan that addresses needs you have identified.

It is important to remember as you read that this chapter gives a big picture view of effective teaching. Teaching methodologies change with certain age groups; it is important to learn how to communicate effectively with whomever you teach. Working with preschool children will require different skills than teaching single adults. Communicating with senior adult is very different than teaching seniors in high school. However, the principles taught in this chapter can be applied to any age group.

Finding The Right Combination

It's never enough to just identify the problem. So the next question we must tackle is "How can I make my teaching more relevant?" Relevant teaching is much more than finding interesting topics about which people are interested in hearing. Relevant teaching is not about different literature, discussion groups, or story telling. Relevant teaching is simply taking God's Word and allowing the truth contained in it to be the catalyst for life-change in the people we teach. When you think about relevant teaching, think about the end product being transformed lives.

Here are some ideas that will help you better understand where relevant teaching comes from.

Relevant teaching comes from God's Word.

All Scripture is inspired by God and is useful to teach us what is true and to make us realize what is wrong in our lives. It corrects us when we are wrong and teaches us to do what is right. God uses it to prepare and equip his people to do every good work.
2 Timothy 3:16

The Bible is the foundation on which all teaching should be based. God's truth found in His Scriptures is as applicable today as it was on the day it was first written. Too many times our teaching begins with our quarterly curriculum or other teaching guide. Why not start with the Bible?

Have you ever planted a garden? It takes a lot of work to have a successful garden. You must have the right soil, the right amount of sunlight, and the proper amount of water. You need adequate space and time for your garden to produce fruit. But do you know what is most important? It's the seed! Without the seed, a garden may look nice, but it will never produce any fruit. Is your teaching like this garden? Don't forget that the seed of God's Word is the most important element to your teaching.

Evaluation Question: Did my teaching today rely upon God's Word in such a way that it was the centerpiece of the lesson?

Relevant teaching characterizes God's Heart.

Dear friends, let us continue to love one another, for love comes from God. Anyone who loves is a child of God and knows God. But anyone who does not love does not know God, for God is love.
1 John 4:7-8

The last thing I do every morning once I've gotten ready is look in the mirror and make sure everything is okay. How does my hair look? Is there anything stuck in my teeth? Do these clothes go together? I don't do this because of vanity or pride, but simply to make sure I have an accurate representation of my condition that day. Sometimes I wish things looked different in the mirror! And as much as I tell the mirror that this or that needs to change, the mirror has no control over my condition. It is simply reflecting who I am. We should strive to be a mirror of God's heart in our teaching.

The goal of our teaching time is not to communicate how we feel about a specific topic or passage of scripture. The goal is to communicate how God feels about it. It is key to remember that this is God's Word to his people, and the teacher's role is to help communicate His words, thoughts and deeds in such a way that people are drawn to a personal relationship with Him.

Evaluation Question: Did my teaching today communicate a characteristic of God in such a way that people were drawn to Him?

Relevant teaching connects with both the mind and the soul.

> *Therefore, go and make disciples of all the nations, baptizing them in the name of the Father and the Son and the Holy Spirit. Teach these new disciples to obey all the commands I have given you.*
>
> *Matthew 28:19-20*

As a teacher, it is easy to get caught in the trap of viewing success as simply passing along information. Although it is important for your class to know the Bible and understand background, history, word origins and meanings, this is not the end result. Simply passing on information does not engage the soul in learning. Teachers should strive to not only educate their class on God's Word, but to also inspire them to seek after God with all their hearts.

I could simply describe my wife to you in terms of height, weight, hair color, eye color, skin tone and history, and you would know about my wife. But I would not have given you a complete picture of who she really is. To hear me talk about my wife you would begin to learn how she loves, how she cares, what makes her angry, what makes her sad, and what is so compelling about her that you couldn't wait to meet her. In our teaching we must engage both the mind and the soul of our learners.

Evaluation Question: Did my teaching today not only communicate the truth of God's Word effectively but also challenge the soul to desire God more?

Relevant teaching communicates direction and meaning.

> *You have heard me teach things that have been confirmed by many reliable witnesses. Now teach these truths to other trustworthy people who will be able to pass them on to others.*
>
> *2 Timothy 2:2*

I remember when I was learning how to drive. The mechanics of the car became very important to me. I needed to know how to start the engine, how to put the car in drive or reverse, how to make the car go and stop, how to turn on the blinkers, lights and windshield wipers, how to park, even parallel park! All of these are important to driving a car. But probably the most important thing about driving a car is knowing where you are going.

Our teaching is the same way, if we know the mechanics but not the direction we lack something very important. We teach people about the faith. We teach them about love and grace. We teach them about forgiveness and mercy. We teach them about discipleship and evangelism. But we never give them a direction in which to go. The goal of teaching is not to keep people in the classroom. The goal of relevant teaching is for people to actually begin to use the knowledge and desires they have developed to make a difference for Christ in this world. Sometimes the way we teach is a lot like the Daytona 500. People are driving but they aren't really going anywhere.

Evaluation Question: Did my teaching today give people an application or direction to follow in order to honor God with their lives?

Relevant teaching causes life transformation.

> *Because of the privilege and authority God has given me, I give each of you this warning: Don't think you are better than you really are. Be honest in your evaluation of yourselves, measuring yourselves by the faith God has given us.*
>
> *Romans 12:3*

The other day I was watching a movie. It was a good movie. I enjoyed the time I spent watching it. I laughed, I cried, I spent $10! Later that week a friend of mine asked me about the movie I saw. The crazy thing was, I couldn't even remember the title, much less the plot. It took me a few minutes to recall what the movie was about and why I had thought it was so good. I realized that although I had enjoyed the movie, it had little or no lasting impact upon me. Why not? Maybe because the movie simply entertained me. The movie didn't ask me to make any changes in my life. It didn't challenge me to obtain goals that I had set. It didn't point out areas of my life that were lacking and motivate me to deal with them. It was simply a good movie.

Maybe you can teach a good lesson. A lesson that makes people laugh, cry and even pay $10! But does your teaching move past entertaining and move toward life transformation? God's Word has authority. That authority exercised in our life causes change. Life transformation happens when we help people come into contact with God's Word through teaching, discussion and application.

Evaluation Question: Did my teaching, through the authority of God's Word, produce lasting life change in those that experienced it?

Breaking Through: How Healthy Sunday Schools Utilize Teaching That Is Relevant to the Audience

I didn't get the chicken pox until my senior year in high school. It was not a time in my life that I would want to relive. When I was first diagnosed with the chicken pox the doctors told my parents to isolate me because I was so contagious. As a matter of fact the older you are when you contract chicken pox the stronger and more contagious they are. For the first couple of days I was stuck in my room with very limited visitors. And then something strange began to happen. Friends and neighbors with small children began to come by and visit and wanted their children to be around me so that their children would be exposed to chicken pox. Over that week, I began to feel a strange sense of popularity because of my sickness. I had something that other people wanted and all they had to do was be in close proximity to me to receive it. As I think back on those days it reminds me of how easy it is to reproduce things in your life in the lives of others.

Relevant effective teaching is much more desirable than chicken pox. But it can be just as contagious.

> *"When teachers begin to grow and become more effective new things begin to be produced in their classes and their churches."*

Just like there are some definite symptoms of the chicken pox, a church and Sunday School that are committed to relevant, effective teaching will show the following results:

- **Sunday Schools that have relevant teaching produce more devoted followers of Christ.**
  When your teaching becomes more relevant and effective you will see true life change happening to those in your class. One of those life changes will show when people begin to take ownership of their faith. Relevant teaching weans people off of the need to receive all their spiritual training from others and helps them connect with God on their own. This in turn moves them toward becoming more effective in their personal evangelism and service.

Evaluation Question: Has our class seen members taking ownership of their faith and expressing it through serving others?

- **Sunday Schools that have relevant teaching produce more new believers and baptisms.**
  Relevant teaching can't help but challenge people to become more evangelistic and by doing so your class will have the opportunity to reach more people than ever before. And once you have some non-believers coming to your class the ever-relevant gospel will impact their lives.

Evaluation Question: Has our class seen at least two people come to know Christ and follow Him in baptism?

- **Sunday Schools that have relevant teaching produce more leaders.**
  When I was a kid my grandparents gave me a substantial monetary gift of $1,000. As an eight year old that seemed like more money than I could ever spend. However there was a condition on the gift that it would have to stay in the bank until I was 18 years old. I couldn't imagine why that money just

had to sit there. Over the years I found many things that I wanted to spend that money on, but could not because the money wasn't available. When I finally turned 18 I was excited to go and get my $1,000. As you probably already know, something special had happened to that $1,000. It had more than doubled in value over those 10 years. I learned a valuable lesson that day. Money invested in the right way reproduces itself. Over the years I've learned the same is true of people. Time and energy invested in people reproduces itself over time.

Leaders are not found; they are developed. Relevant teaching helps the potential leaders who are sitting in your class to move toward fulfilling that potential. Relevant teaching doesn't produce just smarter, more enlightened Christians, but it produces Christians that are moving toward embracing their giftedness and accomplishing effective ministry for Christ.

Evaluation Question: How many leaders has our class produced in the last year? Who am I personally investing in to help them develop their leadership potential?

- **Sunday Schools that have relevant teaching produce more classes.**
Relevant teaching doesn't just produce new leaders it also produces new classes for those new leaders to own. As your Sunday School teachers become more effective in communicating God's truth it will have an effect on enrollment, attendance and giving.

Evaluation Question: Has our class been intentional in helping to birth a new class this year?

- **Sunday Schools that have relevant teaching produce more healthy churches.**
Teaching that is focused on God's Word and people committed to living it out will have an overall impact on your church's health. Whether you know it or not, relevancy and effectiveness of your teaching has a direct impact on your church. If your class is experiencing unity and growth, your church will benefit. If your class is characteristically unhealthy, you'll have a negative impact on your church.

Evaluation Question: Has our class helped to maintain the unity of our church by moving the focus off of ourselves and onto reaching and connecting with others?

Ten Key Ideas That You Can Use

1. *Develop a Preparation Plan.* Determine when your schedule allows you preparation time and schedule it into your week. If you don't have a preparation plan, you'll end up preparing at the last minute. When you plan at the last minute you might be able to do an adequate job of teaching but you will have missed the opportunity to be the most effective teacher you can.

2. *Get to know each of the learners in your class.* Everyone in your class has different learning styles. We tend to think this just applies to children and teenagers, but adults maintain different learning styles as well. Some people in your class will be visual learners, other will need hands-on experience, and still others learn best just by listening. Try to identify how the people in your class learn and develop different parts of your lesson that will connect with each style.

3. *Use a variety of teaching methods.* Even the most creative methods of teaching get boring if they are repeated every week. There is nothing wrong with using your natural teaching style on a regular basis. But look for opportunities to stretch yourself and your class. If you are a lecturer, then occasionally divide the class into discussion groups. If you are more of an interactive teacher, then occasionally have a guest come in who can bring a focused talk on a specific subject. Variety is the spice of life and it can add spice to your teaching as well.

4. *Record yourself teaching and evaluate yourself.* I'll begin by telling you this is not fun. Most of us are our worst critics, and to sit and listen to yourself teach can be agonizing. But it can also be very insightful. When we listen to ourselves we can find ways to improve and stretch ourselves. It's as simple as getting a tape recorder and sitting it in the corner while you speak.

5. *Have someone sit in on your class and evaluate your teaching.* An outside ear can be a great asset in evaluating your teaching. When you ask someone to evaluate you, you must give them the freedom to be honest with you. Let them know that you want to know what can be improved, not simply what they enjoyed. It's important to find someone that has experience teaching and has the boldness to be honest with you. Don't fall into the temptation to let the criticism upset you, instead let it challenge you to grow.

6. *Find a teaching mentor and someone to mentor.* No matter how long you have been teaching there is someone out there better than you. It's important to find someone that will help you grow and develop as a teacher. Ask them to help you with specific areas like preparation and presentation styles. It's also important for you to find someone in whom you can invest your experience. As we teach others, we in turn become sharper.

7. *Look for training opportunities to become a more effective teacher.* It's important that every year you attend some training to become a more effective teacher. The Sunday School/Open Groups Ministry office provides training throughout the year; there are other opportunities available as well. The important thing is to take advantage of training opportunities.

8. *Evaluate your class size regularly to make sure you keep proper leader to learner ratios.* Even the best teachers can loose effectiveness if their class size becomes to big or too small. Check the appropriate ratio for the age you teach. If your class is becoming too large begin to mentor another teacher to birth a new class.

9. *Read at least one book a year on becoming a better teacher.* There are numerous books available that will help you become a better teacher. Develop a reading plan that includes different authors and topics. The best thing a teacher can do is to continue to be a learner.

10. *Pray for wisdom in your teaching.* Life transforming teaching can only come from God. Our biggest strength is the wisdom and power of God, and it is ours for the asking.

> "Never begin to teach with out asking God to communicate through you."

KEY #7

SPACE IS PROVIDED FOR GROWTH

Unlocking The Purpose of Space

Enlarge the place of your tent, stretch your tent curtains wide, do not hold back; lengthen your cords, strengthen your stakes.

Isaiah 54:2

Providing excellent quality and the appropriate quantity of Sunday School space is a crucial element in planning for the growth of your Sunday School. Knowing your Sunday School space potential and limitations will assist in planning for future growth, for use of facilities, and for additional facilities. It takes work and a willingness to "shake things up" in order for this to be accomplished. In considering Sunday School space, you need to understand the purpose of space, how to effectively use existing space, and how to plan for future space.

Arthur Flake first published <u>Building a Standard Sunday School</u> in 1922 and it became the foundation leading to 75 years of growth using the Sunday School as an entry point for worship service growth. "Provide the space" was the third of Flake's original five points, which eventually became known as "Flake's Fivefold Formula" for church growth. In his book, Flake wrote, "There is no such thing as building a Sunday School great in numbers in small, cramped quarters."

Flake lists two things that need to happen in order to provide a suitable place in which to build and maintain a great Sunday School.

1. **Present Quarters Should Be Adjusted.**
   In planning to increase the growth of the Sunday School, it is often necessary to readjust the arrangement of the building. Often an adult class is meeting in a large room when a much smaller room would serve its purpose. Frequently there is not enough room in the present quarters and outside space should be secured. A public school building nearby may be secured for one or more classes or entire departments. Often a temporary building may be erected close by the

church building to take care of one or more departments or one or more classes. Again let it be said that a large Sunday School cannot be built and maintained in small, cramped quarters; and sane, sensible arrangements should be made for the expansion of the Sunday School.

2. New Buildings Should Be Erected.
Many Sunday Schools have to 'swarm' before the church membership realizes that a larger, better-equipped building is needed. Hundreds and even thousands of our church houses in the Southland are wholly inadequate from the standpoint of size and proper adjustment to take care of the Sunday Schools the churches should have. There is no economy in a church maintaining a small, inefficient Sunday School when there are multitudes of people all around who could be won into the Sunday School if adequate quarters were provided."

While these principles still hold true, the application of these principles has changed. In The Book of Church Growth, Thom S. Rainer states, "Flake's fivefold method of growth continues to be effective. It is still one of the essential keys to healthy Sunday School!" Providing space is a key which can and will lead to a healthy and growing Sunday School.

Churches often find themselves in difficult situations concerning the use of space in their facilities for Sunday School. Two popular quotes relating to space sum up these situations: from the original Star Trek television series "Space, the final frontier... to boldly go where no man has gone before!" and from the Apollo Thirteen crisis "Houston, we have a problem." Like men in space, today's Sunday Schools have to learn to overcome these challenges.

"Space, the final frontier...to boldly go where no man has gone before!" There are some churches today that are using their Sunday School space the same way that it has been used since the building was constructed. To change the present use of these rooms is a place where no one has ever dared to go. The possibility of a different, more effective use of space is a new, never before explored frontier. As a Sunday School leader, you need to boldly go into this territory. Make whatever changes are necessary to ensure that the best possible use of space is accomplished.

The use of Sunday School space is a challenging frontier for all churches. Some churches have moved into this new frontier and conquered it with amazing growth into the "new" spaces. Others have become paralyzed by these challenges, afraid to try something new. While others are satisfied to stay the same size and leave things just as they are. The challenge of conquering the Sunday School space frontier is an important key to having an effective and healthy Sunday School ministry.

In a recent study of Georgia's Fastest Growing Sunday Schools by Sunday School/Open Group Ministries of the Georgia Baptist Convention, it was determined that these churches overwhelmingly have traveled into and conquered this space frontier. Dr. Steve Parr, Vice President for Sunday School and Evangelism, relates the attitudes of these churches concerning space:

> "The members make sacrifices by meeting in less than desirable settings if needed in order to sustain growth. The focus is on reaching the community. Schedules and room assignments are not held sacred in these churches. People are willing to change rooms, locations, and meeting times in order for more people to be reached for Christ and included in Bible Study."

"Houston, we have a problem," astronaut Jack Swigert radioed after he noticed a warning light accompanied by an explosion aboard the Apollo 13 spacecraft. Today, many churches are noticing a warning light as well. They are concerned about their use of space for Sunday School and are crying out, "Help, we have a problem here." These churches have reached a level of growth and ministry where continued growth is prohibited because of the lack of space or inefficient or ineffective use of existing space.

The more wisely you use the space you have, the more efficient and effective you will be in providing the best environment for accomplishing the purpose of the Sunday School. Peter Drucker says, "Efficiency is doing things right, and effectiveness is doing the right things!" In providing Sunday School space you have to be both efficient and effective! Some churches use their space effectively and efficiently and have reached their fullest potential with existing space; they are literally "spaced out." The space crunch can be a problem, or it can be the start of a great opportunity! Encarta defines space as "an area set apart: an area set apart or available for use." Some churches are blessed with more space than they will ever be able to adequately use. Other congregations are struggling with adequate space, but the space is not "set apart" in an effective manner. Still others have "set apart" all the space they can and still are busting at the seams. They are using every possible area for education and worship, and are totally "maxed" out. The diverse challenges that each of these churches face can be overcome.

The key to unlocking your space is to understand the purpose of the Sunday School space and to use that space in order to accomplish its purpose. The driving force of the Sunday School is the Great Commission. We are to be obedient to go, to make disciples, to baptize, and to teach. Remember, according to <u>Sunday School for a New Century</u>, Sunday School is "the foundational strategy in a local church for leading people to faith in the Lord Jesus Christ, and building Great Commission Christians through Bible study groups, which engage people in evangelism, discipleship, ministry, fellowship and worship."

> *"You should provide space in order to reach people, make disciples, and to carry out the basic functions of the church."*

Davis Byrd, of LifeWay's Church Architecture Department, says, "The purpose of the church is not a church building, but church building." How are you using the church building in order to build the church?

In the book, <u>When Not to Build: An Architect's Unconventional Wisdom for the Growing Church</u>, Ray Bowman and Ernie Hall state, "If the church's mission is to minister to people in Christ's name, church buildings can have only one legitimate function: to serve as tools to help church members fulfill that mission. If our focus is truly on people rather than buildings, that reality will shape the kinds of buildings we design, how we use them, how much we spend on them, and how much time, energy, and money we keep free for the real work of the church: meeting people's needs."

Winston Churchill once said, "We shape our buildings, then they shape us!" Billy Britt, Pastor of Ministries at Hebron Baptist Church in Dacula, Georgia, challenges churches to "not let the building determine your ministry, rather, let your ministry determine your building." Bob Lunn, Director of Commercial Development at the design-build firm Barden & Robeson, supports this, saying, "People are not attracted by beautiful buildings but by meaningful ministry. The building is just the tool of the ministry. It is not the ministry, as so many churches think." You build or expand to meet the needs of the ministry, not to make a ministry. Once again, the authors of When Not to Build state, "The experience of the Jerusalem church demonstrates a powerful truth: We may think a congregation can't grow until the church building has more square feet, but the real limiting factor is not the building; it's how we think about and use the building." Are you willing to have a "whatever it takes" attitude in order for the church to fully reach its potential and in order to reach your community for Christ?

Finding the Right Combination

Providing an adequate amount of quality education space is vital in order for the Sunday School to grow. How much space is needed for Sunday School? The recommended ratio is to have one class or unit for every ten people in average attendance. For example, if your average Sunday School attendance is 200, then you should have at least 20 classes. The actual square footage of these rooms will determine the average attendance capacity of that particular room.

According the Ken Hemphill, "The building functions simply as a container for the church. The container can either restrict or facilitate growth." A church can do all the right things and still not grow because "the pot" is too small. Hemphill also states that, "A small building can limit a church from growing to the natural size for its community." The size of "the pot" or the building will determine attendance. This is a concept that many churches have a hard time accepting. Their pot is too small and they either do not recognize the problem or they are unwilling to get a larger pot!

> *"Churches that think they are running out of room often are surprised to learn that they can double or triple in size without a major building program simply by changing how they think about and use their present space. Until a church fully utilizes its existing building, a need for more space does not exist."*
> When Not to Build: An Architect's Unconventional Wisdom for the Growing Church

Following are some ways suggested by Ray Bowman and Ernie Hall to solve space problems without new facilities:

- Move groups to the right size rooms.
- Change the group size to fit the room.
- Change furniture.
- Use creative scheduling.
- Consider what minor remodeling can do.
- Build or rent a storage building.
- Find new uses for any space not already fully used.

Knowing the amount of space required for effective ministry for each age group is crucial to providing space for growth. A church needs to provide the best possible space for small-group Bible study. Also, function is the most important characteristic for a church educational building. A building may be attractive and impressive, but if it is not functional its basic purpose will not be fulfilled. Before thinking about concrete, brick, lumber, and dollars, the church needs to develop, on the basis of good research, a list of specific program space needs for each age group and department. A functional building plan should be designed to meet those needs adequately. The following suggestions, adapted from Sunday School for a New Century, will assist you in determining the most effective use of space.

- Analyze all available space using the recommended guidelines provided.
- Determine the total square footage of space available that can be used by Bible study groups.
- Determine the square footage needed by all the Sunday School departments and classes in all age groups.
- Based on community changes and age group shifts, determine whether more space is needed or whether reallocation of space is an option.
- What is a reasonable projection of enrollment, average attendance, and growth for each of the age groups over the next growth cycle?
- How should groups be organized in terms of ages, departments, and classes?
- Where should the age group spaces be located, and what should be the relationships between the various spaces?
- How do people get to and from these areas in terms of movement, access, convenience, safety, and emergency?

- What kinds of support spaces are needed beyond department and classrooms?
- Determine whether any additional space is available for church use (by the purchase or lease of portable buildings or other nearby buildings).
- Determine whether multiple use of space is a possibility.
- Are there special considerations, such as a day-care program, multiple scheduling of Sunday School, or multiple uses for certain spaces?
- Evaluate whether a new building is a priority.
- If there are existing buildings, how can they best be used in combination with new buildings?

Assessing the church's physical space will help you determine what your maximum attendance capacity is. The maximum attendance capacity of a room is determined by the square footage of the room divided by the square footage needed for each age group (samples follow).

Education Space:
Formula: square footage x 45 square feet per person. You can expect to average 80% of this figure.

Sunday School Classrooms:
Preschool: 35 square feet per person
Children: 25 square feet per person
Youth: 18 square feet per person
Adults: 18 square feet per person

Worship:
Maximum Attendance Capacity = Total number of inches of pews divided by 21 plus the seating capacity of the platform and the choir.

Average Attendance Capacity = Pew seating capacity x 80% plus seating capacity of the platform and choir.

Fellowship:
Divide the total square footage of the fellowship space by 15 (if round tables are used) or 12 (if rectangular tables are used). Adequate fellowship space should be one-half to one-third of the education space.

KEY Strategies - FOR HEALTHY SUNDAY SCHOOLS

Parking:
There needs to be one space for every 2-2.5 people in attendance on site at one time.

Land:
Count on 100 people per acre for maximum one time attendance capacity. If multi-level buildings are used you can count on 125 people per acre.

The 80% rule comes into play significantly when you are determining what the building can accommodate in attendance. A room can generally accommodate an average attendance of 80% of its total maximum capacity. Ken Hemphill says that, "When any portion of the building is 80% filled, the church's natural growth will be inhibited and finally stopped." Maximum attendance capacity is determined based on the square footage minimum requirements for each age group.

Breaking Through: How Healthy Sunday Schools Utilize Space

> *Solomon wrote, "Any enterprise is built by wise planning, becomes strong through common sense, and profits wonderfully by keeping abreast of the facts"*
> *(Prov. 24:3-4 LB).*

Davis Byrd notes that studies of growing churches consistently show that property, buildings, and space are major factors in sustaining growth patterns. In the Sunday School Growth Plan, Tim S. Smith says, "You must have adequate space in order to grow! However, do not let the lack of space limit your potential. If you fill parking, worship, or educational space you will stop growth from occurring." If you are looking at the space frontier and shaking your head in defeat because you feel you can't grow, please do not give up! You may have to really be creative and try some things you thought would never be possible. Ask yourself the question, "What am I willing to do in order to provide more space in order to reach more people?" Remember the quote from Gene Kranz, flight director for Apollo 13, "Failure is not an option!" The crew of Apollo 13 and the support crew at Mission Control worked as hard as they could to come up with a solution to bring those astronauts back home. Nothing was out-of-bounds or off limits! They came up with solutions that they never would have imagined would be possible or necessary! Do you have this attitude? Does your church?

In order to determine your present space capabilities, you need to determine what the Maximum Sunday School Attendance (MSSA) capacity is, then take 80% of the MSSA capacity to find the Average Sunday School Attendance (ASSA) capacity. You will need to do a comprehensive study of your entire property and facility. This study should include the answer to these questions:

1. What is the square footage of each room used for Sunday School?
2. What age group currently meets in each room?
3. What is the present enrollment and average attendance for each class?
4. Which rooms are not presently used? What is the square footage for those rooms?
5. What is the total length, in inches, of the pews?
6. How many identifiable parking spaces currently exist?
7. What is the total acreage owned by the church (not including land used for a cemetery)?

All of these are important factors in determining the present attendance capability and are the beginning point for making projections for the need of future space.

Balance worship space with education space. An indication of a healthy and growing church is when average worship attendance is 10-20% more than Sunday School attendance. The church needs to plan on providing enough Sunday School space in order to meet this ratio. How is this calculated?

Step 1: Multiply the average attendance capacity of your worship facility by .20 then multiply that number by 4.166. This will give you the target Sunday School attendance number for which you need to provide.

▶ For example, if your average worship attendance capacity is 300:
  - 300 x .20 = 60
  - 60 x 4.166 = 250
  - If you have worship space to average 300, then you need to provide Sunday School space to average 250.

▶ If you want to provide space to average 250, this will be 80% of your MSSA capacity. To figure the MSSA capacity, divide the ASSA capacity desired by 80%.

- For example: If average attendance desired in Sunday School is 250:
- 250 ÷ .80 = 313
- This is the number of people that you need to provide space for in Sunday School.

Step 2: Once the amount of education space is determined, you will then need to determine how much space is needed for each age group. It is recommended that the attendance percentages for each age group should be approximately:

- Adults   55%
- Youth   15%
- Children   15%
- Preschool 15%

▶ Take the maximum attendance number you just figured and multiply by the appropriate percentages per age group.

- Example: MSSA is 313.
  Adults: 313 x 55% = 172
  Youth: 313 x 15% = 47
  Children: 313 x 15% = 47
  Preschool: 313 x 15% = 47
  Total   = **313**

Step 3: Take the MSSA figure for each group and multiply that number by the appropriate square footage required for each age group.

- Adult: 18 square feet per person
- Youth: 18 square feet per person
- Children: 25 square feet per person
- Preschool: 35 square feet per person

Example:
Adults: 172 x 18 = 3,094 square feet
Youth: 47 x 18 = 844
Children: 47 x 25 = 1,172
Preschool: 47 x 35 = 1,641
Total   6,750 square feet

Step 4: To determine the number of classes needed per age group, take the ASSA number and divide it by the recommended average per class for each age group. The recommended averages are:

- Adults: 12-15 per class
- Youth: 10 per class
- Children: 10 per class
- Preschool: 7 per class

This chart reflects the findings of the previous steps.

AGE GROUP	MSSA	ASSA	SQUARE FOOTAGE		CLASSROOMS
ADULT	172	137	172 x 18 sq. = 3094	11	12 per adult class
YOUTH	47	37	47 x 18 sq. = 844	5	10 youth per class
CHILDREN	47	37	47 x 25 sq. = 1172	4	10 children per class
PRESCHOOL	47	37	47 x 35 sq. = 1641	5	7 preschooler per class
TOTAL	**313**	**250**	**Total Sq. Ft. = 6750**	**25**	**25 x 10 = 250**

Ten Key Ideas That You Can Use

1. *Think with a SPACE mindset.*
   Support the overall work of the Sunday School by providing space.

   Provide the best available space for preschool and children. Preschoolers should be on the main floor. When the preschool area is out of space, you need to consider yourself totally out of space even though there may be some unused space for other age groups.

   Anticipate future educational space needs and challenges and address them.

   Commit to an attitude of "whatever it takes" in using all available space for Sunday School.

   Evaluate space usage annually to ensure the most effective and efficient use of all available space.

2. *Divide large meeting areas with portable or permanent partitions.* See resources for contact information on Screenflex Portable Partitions and Versipanels.

3. *Utilize portable trailer units.* Trailers can be leased or purchased. Contact your local school board to get recommendations on trailer leasing companies.

4. *Make sure all available space is used.* This includes any space that can accommodate a Sunday School class.

   "No space should be off limits."

   This includes: sanctuary, choir room, large corridor areas, kitchen, offices, library, conference room, and baptismal dressing rooms. Topper Reid, of the Hunter Street Baptist Church in Birmingham, AL and Dr. Randy Millwood, of the Baptist Convention of Maryland/Delaware submitted the following suggestions for creative use of space

   ❏ Three Sunday School Hours
   ❏ Aerobics Room

- ❏ Gym...Screen Flex a quarter of gym off
- ❏ Brides Room
- ❏ Use Screen Flex to create rooms for Sunday School in large open areas
- ❏ Game Room in Gym
- ❏ Snack area in Gym
- ❏ Serving Room in Kitchen
- ❏ Sound Room in Chapel
- ❏ Sunday School Literature Room
- ❏ Sunday School Records Office
- ❏ Construction Trailer on site
- ❏ Office cubicles
- ❏ Unused Preschool room for adults
- ❏ Off Campus
- ❏ Doctor's waiting room for adult class
- ❏ Real Estate office for Singles class
- ❏ Apartment Club room for young married
- ❏ Lease office space for Sunday School
- ❏ Homes in the adjoining neighborhoods with classes of young singles (no kids involved) or middle-aged adults (kids in youth group or older)
- ❏ Use standing, rolling chalkboards to create classroom space at the ends of halls
- ❏ Offices, library, etc.
- ❏ Stairwells (seating classes of 8-10 or less on ascending stairs with the teacher at the bottom - youth and young adults)
- ❏ Church buses (temporarily and in spring/fall)
- ❏ Restroom (again, temporarily)

5. *Check with local businesses.* It may be possible to use their space or even rent space from them for Sunday School. This could also include a school, community clubhouse, neighborhood clubhouse, even a church member's home.

6. *Make the best use of space.* Are small classes in larger classrooms? Are larger classes in smaller rooms? Make sure that the rooms are used according to size needs.

7. *The use of tables in adult and youth classrooms lessens the attendance capacity of that room.* Encourage classes to remove tables from the room in order to make better use of space.

8. *Develop a "shared use of space" agreement with all class leaders.* This will include an understanding that the use of space will fluctuate in order to provide the best possible use of space. There is no guarantee that any classroom space will be permanent. This will prevent the "we shall not be moved" mentality from occurring.

9. *Multiple Sunday School meeting times.* When the physical facilities and resources are not enough to accommodate the number of people attending Sunday School at the same time, and all other options have been exhausted, then you should consider multiple Sunday School hours.

10. *Request a Church Building Consultation from your State Convention.* This is a service available in most states at no cost.

Resources:

EDUCATIONAL FACILITIES:
Rules of Thumb for Effective Sunday School

General Building Size:
(Education, fellowship, administration, music, media, with some multi-purpose space.)

First Unit Building: 30-40 square feet per person
Small Churches: 40-45 square feet per person
Large Churches with extensive programs: 45-55 square feet per person

MINIMUM SQUARE FOOTAGE REQUIREMENTS FOR CLASSROOMS:

Age Group	Space Per Person	Room Capacity	Room Size	Multi-purpose Space
Preschool				
Birth to 1		7	292 sq. ft. minimum	
2 Year	35 sq. ft. recommended	9	665 sq. ft. maximum	
3-5 Year		12	No walls less than 12 ft.	
Children			325 sq. ft. minimum	
Grade 1-6	25 sq. ft. recommended	10	650 sq. ft. maximum	
Youth			144 sq. ft. minimum	22 sq. ft. per person
Grade 7-12	18 sq. ft. recommended	10	270 sq. ft. maximum	recommended
Adult			270 sq. ft. minimum	22 sq. ft. per person
Age 18 and up	18 sq. ft. recommended	12-15	450 sq. ft. maximum	recommended

Local Architect, Contact your State Convention for Church Vendor List

Screenflex Portable Partitions, 1-800-553-0110, www.screenflex.com

Versipanels, www.versipanel.com. 11225 N. 28th Dr., Suite D-122, Phoenix, AZ 85029, 602-942-4841, 877-942-4841 toll-free, 602-942-4899 fax

Bowman, Ray & Eddy Hall, <u>When Not to Build: An Architect's Unconventional Wisdom for the Growing Church</u>, Grand Rapids, Baker.

Powers, Bruce B. editor, <u>Church Administration Handbook</u>, Nashville, Broadman & Holman Publishers, 1997.

McCormick, Gwenn E., <u>Planning and Building Church Facilities</u>, Nashville, Broadman Press, 1992.

McCormick, Gwenn E., <u>Designing Worship Centers</u>, Nashville, Convention Press, 1988.

Lowry, Robert N., <u>Designing Education Buildings</u>, Nashville, Convention Press, 1990.

Web Resources:

Church Facilities Department, Baptist General Convention of Texas, (214) 828-5125 or e-mail churchfacilities@bgct.org, 333 N. Washington Ave. Dallas, TX 75246, www.bgct.org/churchfacilities/publications.htm

ChristianityToday.Com, www.christianitytoday.com/cbg/

ChurchBuyersGuide.Com, www.churchbuyersguide.com

Church Architecture, A Service of LifeWay Church Resources, A Division of LifeWay Christian Resources. Phone: 615-251-2466, Email: carch@lifeway.com Web page: http://www.lifeway.com/churcharchitecture/index.htm

KEY #8

THERE IS A PLAN FOR OUTREACH

Unlocking The Purpose Of Outreach

All of the key strategies are vitally important, but the one that is absolutely essential is outreach. From the earliest days of God's dealings with humanity, He has told His people to go out and bring others in (Deut. 31:12). Jesus repeated this command to His followers (Luke 10:1; Matt. 28:19). Outreach was a major endeavor of the early church (Acts 2:46-47). Effective organization, training, and space are vitally important, but they are useless unless the Sunday School makes a conscious commitment and takes definite actions in the area of outreach.

What is outreach? The term "outreach" is used in many different ways in our churches. To define the term appropriately, consider what outreach is not. Hospital visitation is not outreach, unless the person you are visiting is a prospect. Visiting Sunday School class members is not outreach, neither is ministry visitation to your own members. Taking food to a church family when a death has occurred is appropriate, but that is not outreach (taking food to a prospect family, however, would be outreach). Most churches will put the words "Y'all Come" or "You're Invited" on the church sign, but that is advertisement, not outreach. Sending postcards and making phone calls to your class members is a wonderful ministry, but that is not outreach. In reality, many church activities that get lumped under the heading of outreach are actually ministry related efforts directed toward church members.

What, then, is outreach? Outreach may be defined as *intentionally reaching out to people who are not members of your Sunday School, so they can come under the teaching of God's Word and be saved.*

You can easily determine whether an activity is truly outreach, by examining its object and purpose. The object of outreach should be those who are not members of the Sunday School. The purpose of outreach is the salvation of the lost. In other words, outreach is directed toward those who are outside the Sunday School, and its goal is to expose them to the Bible, so they may come to be saved.

Outreach is a key strategy for a healthy Sunday School because healthy Sunday Schools will, without exception, be heavily involved in outreach. A Sunday School that ignores outreach is not only unhealthy it is actually dead!

Jesus gave the church the task of fulfilling the Great Commission. In Matthew 28:19-20, the Lord said, "Go ye therefore, and teach all nations, baptizing them in the name of the Father, and of the Son, and of the Holy Ghost: Teaching them to observe all things whatsoever I have commanded you: and, lo, I am with you always, even unto the end of the world."

Key #1 focused on the purpose of the Sunday School. Remember that the Sunday School is not a separate organization within the church; rather, it is the entire church organized to effectively carry out the Great Commission. As such, the Great Commission makes up the "marching orders" not only of the church, but also of the Sunday School. The Great Commission clearly states the commandment to go and carry the gospel to everyone. As Jesus said in Mark 16:15, "Go ye into all the world, and preach the gospel to every creature."

One of the major purposes of the Sunday School is to reach out and spread the gospel. Romans 10:17 tells us, "Faith cometh by hearing, and hearing by the word of God." In other words, a lost person must be exposed to the Bible in some form in order to come to salvation. Since the Sunday School is the Bible teaching ministry of the church, it is only natural that it should also be the reaching arm of the church. Exposure to the Word of God leads to salvation, so a healthy Sunday School will be a reaching Sunday School.

Sunday School is like a living organism. Living things never stay the same; they either grow or they die. A child comes home from the hospital weighing only seven pounds and taking only two ounces of milk at each feeding, but that does not last long. Give that child about sixteen years, and he will weigh 150 pounds and eat everything in the refrigerator! If you buy a pretty plant in a decorative pot and take it to your home, that plant will grow, change, and require a bigger pot or it will die. Living things grow and change.

The Sunday School is no different. If your Sunday School is not actively and purposefully involved in outreach, it will dry up and die. A Sunday School that doesn't reach out will soon become self-centered and self-satisfied.

Outreach is so important to the health of a Sunday School that it can be found in every "formula" for Sunday School work produced over the last century. The last and ultimate step in Arthur Flake's famous formula is "go after the people." Dr. J. N. Barnette and Sunday School evangelist Leon Kilbreth popularized the "Seven Laws of Sunday School Growth." The sixth of those laws is the law of visitation, which says, "Average attendance and enrollment will increase in direct proportion to visits made."

The importance of outreach is also evident in "Piland's Nine" and the Sunday School Growth Spiral. The definition of Sunday School in Sunday School For A New Century begins with the words "Sunday School is the foundational strategy in a local church for leading people to faith in the Lord Jesus Christ." Through the FAITH Sunday School Evangelism strategy, many churches have been reminded that a healthy Sunday School is one that reaches out to the lost. The book Ten Best Practices To Make Your Sunday School Work includes elements of outreach in practices two, four, and five.

In summary, a Sunday School cannot be healthy, and ultimately be obedient and pleasing to God, without being actively involved in outreach. Since outreach is so important, the next task is to find the right combination for effective outreach through the Sunday School.

Finding The Right Combination

How should a church evaluate itself in the area of outreach? You cannot chart a course for a trip without knowing two very important facts: your starting place and your destination. The destination for your journey toward a healthy Sunday School is outreach, but what is your starting place? Where is your Sunday School right now, as it relates to outreach? How can a church effectively evaluate itself in the area of outreach? To evaluate your Sunday School, answer the following questions.

1. Does your church have a time of organized outreach on a regular basis? A few Christians will regularly reach out to the lost on their own, but most of us need the encouragement and structure of an organized, church-wide visitation time. If your church does not have a regular time for outreach visitation, then very little outreach is actually occurring. The 2001 study of Georgia's Fastest Growing

Sunday Schools conducted by Sunday School/Open Group Ministries of the Georgia Baptist Convention revealed that 80% of the fastest growing Sunday Schools have a weekly visitation and outreach night.

2. **How many people are actually involved in outreach visitation?** In most churches, the people involved in outreach can be counted on the fingers of one hand, but the Bible tells all Christians to be outreachers. Acts 1:8 does not read: "But [the Pastor, Sunday School Director, and two deacons] shall receive power, after that the Holy Ghost is come upon you: and [the Pastor, Sunday School Director, and two deacons] shall be witnesses unto me both in Jerusalem, and in all Judea, and in Samaria, and unto the uttermost part of the earth." All believers are commanded to reach out and witness, but sadly very few ever obey that command.

3. **Is every Sunday School class represented in outreach visitation?** Again, the Lord did not exempt the senior adults, teachers of infants, or any other age group from the command to reach out. Every Sunday School class or teaching unit should be involved in outreach.

4. **Are there unreached people within driving distance of your church?** If so, then your Sunday School needs to do more about outreach. Many well-meaning Sunday School members will say, "Everyone in our community goes to either the Baptist or the Methodist church." That is simply not true. There are unchurched people all around us. A people search or door-to-door survey will uncover multitudes of people who need the gospel message of salvation that the healthy Sunday School has to offer.

5. **Do you have a comprehensive approach to outreach?** Visitation is not the sole source of effective outreach. Developing a culture of invitation, planning evangelistic events, equipping members in personal evangelism, and helping members discover how to reach out day by day is the ultimate key to effectiveness.

The early church went from house to house, and the Lord added to the church daily (Acts 2:46-47). Modern church members often stay in our houses and hope the Lord will add someone to our church every so often in spite of our inactivity and disobedience.

Every class or teaching unit must be involved for complete and well-balanced outreach to take place. If your Sunday School is age-graded and every class is involved in outreach, then your church will actively reach out to everyone, of every age, in your community. Mothers, fathers, children, preschoolers, youth, and senior adults can all be reached if every Sunday School class becomes involved in outreach.

For effective outreach and evangelism to take place, every Sunday School leader should be involved. Preschool leaders should reach out to preschoolers and their parents. Children's leaders should reach out to children and their parents. Youth Sunday School leaders should reach out to youth and their parents. Adult Sunday School teachers, Outreach Leaders, and Care Group Leaders should busy themselves reaching out to other adults and their families. Sunday School members in the adult, youth, and children's divisions should be encouraged to become involved in outreach. Senior adults are often reluctant to get out of the house and drive after dark, but they can be led to do outreach during the daytime. Every segment of the healthy Sunday School should be involved in outreach!

A great goal for each Sunday School class is to reproduce itself within a one or two year time span. If classes are faithful in outreach, God blesses with results. More classes can then be organized and more leaders can be enlisted. Growth can continue indefinitely!

What happens if every age group is not represented in outreach visitation? The result will be growth in some areas of the Sunday School and stagnation in others, or no growth at all. Remember that the Lord promised His presence and His power (Matt. 28:18-20), but He expects all believers to be engaged in reaching and teaching people. If the church ceases to reach out, it will be dead in a generation. Some churches have neglected this important task, and their membership is aging and dwindling. The church is a living, vibrant organism referred to in scripture as the body of Christ (1 Cor. 12:27; Eph. 4:12). That body must use the tools at hand– the Sunday School and its members– to reach out to the lost.

Breaking Through: How Healthy Sunday Schools Utilize Outreach

The Great Commission, not tradition, drives Healthy Sunday Schools. The phrase "we've never done it that way before" will not be uttered in the healthy Sunday School.

> *"The Great Commission, and its commands to reach out and witness, must be the driving force behind the Sunday School."*

Some Sunday Schools are bound up by so much tradition that they can't obey the Bible and reach out to the lost. If your Sunday School is not reaching people, remember this truth: "If you continue to do what you've always done, then you will continue to get the results you have always gotten." Traditions can be wonderful, but if they are not based on the Bible, then they may be detrimental.

Healthy Sunday Schools are focused on reaching the unreached, not making themselves comfortable. In most churches it is easier to raise money for new carpeting, padded pews, and gymnasiums than for outreach activities, Sunday School supplies, and additional educational space. The Great Commission did not instruct us to make ourselves comfortable but to reach out to the lost. Healthy Sunday Schools focus on reaching the lost.

Healthy Sunday Schools maintain a good balance between outreach to the lost and ministry to their own members. The Lord has commanded the church not only to reach out but also to minister to one another (Gal. 6:2; Rom. 12:15). Outreach and ministry are both important tasks, and neither can be neglected. In a healthy Sunday School, one will not outweigh or receive more emphasis than the other.

Healthy Sunday Schools are obedient to the clear commands of scripture. The Lord has clearly commanded all Christians to be involved in outreach and evangelism (Deut. 31:12; Matt. 28:19-20; Mark 16:15; Acts 1:8). A Sunday School that is neglecting or disobeying these commands cannot expect to be healthy or blessed by God.

Sunday School is the outreach arm of a healthy church. In a healthy church, all outreach is channeled through and tied into the Sunday School. The Sunday School is the ideal reaching arm for the church because it involves more church members than any other organization. It is organized for effective outreach and is equipped to properly assimilate the new people who join.

Healthy Sunday Schools seek to enroll lost people. The best place on earth for a lost person to be is on the roll of an evangelistic, Bible-teaching Sunday School. The lost person enrolled in such a Sunday School will be prayed for, visited, witnessed to, ministered to, and loved. "Cold call" evangelism (witnessing to someone with whom you don't already have a relationship) is good, but it generally takes over 240 such visits to result in one new convert. On the contrary, if you enroll three lost persons in Sunday School, at least one of them will be saved in a year's time. One out of 240, or one out of three– which result sounds best to you? One of the best, but least utilized, methods of winning the lost is to enroll them in Sunday School and then love them, pray for them, minister to them, and teach them. Healthy Sunday Schools do this.

Healthy Sunday Schools have an outreach leader in every adult Sunday School class. Andy Anderson once said that outreach is like the gas pedal on a car. If you continue to push the gas pedal, the car will continue to go. If you take your foot off the gas pedal, the car will slow and eventually come to a stop. Christians need constant reminders and encouragement to be involved in outreach. That task falls to the Outreach Leader in the adult Sunday School class. He or she should keep outreach constantly before the class and do everything possible to get all class members involved.

A healthy Sunday School results in a healthy church. As the Sunday School goes, so goes the church. Remember that the Sunday School is not a separate and independent organization; it is the church, organized to perform its Great Commission functions. If the Sunday School is healthy, the church will be healthy. Leaders should strive to make Sunday School the best it can possibly be because the future of our church depends on it.

Ten Key Ideas That You Can Use

1. *Organize (or start) your prospect file.* Your Sunday School needs a well-organized prospect file. People become discouraged and may even stop going on visitation if there are not sufficient prospects to keep them busy. If you do not have a prospect file, begin one. Do you have a stack of old visitor cards stored somewhere in the church office? Is there a database of prospects or a box of prospect cards from

some past people search? Locate that information, organize it, update it, and put it to work. Business experts say that information is power, and the more information you have about prospects, the better your chances of making a positive impact on them. Prospect information can be organized in a card file or on a computer. Regardless of the method, you should have each prospect's name, address, telephone number, date of birth, and spiritual condition. Prospect information should be kept for each individual, but there should also be a way to cross-reference the other family members of each prospect. You should assign each prospect to his or her proper Sunday School class, and have a way of keeping track of visits and contacts made to that prospect, along with the results of those contacts.

2. *Look for more prospects.* A healthy Sunday School should have a prospect file of equal or larger size than the Sunday School enrollment. That's a lot of prospects! Where will you find them? First, be sure that every visitor to your Sunday School, worship service, or church activity fills out some type of a visitor card, which asks for the visitor's name, address, phone number, and date of birth. Add those visitors to the prospect file. A second way to find more prospects is to do a door-to-door survey or people search. Go to each home in the community, identify yourself, and ask if the residents have a church home, which they attend regularly. If they don't, ask for their information and add them to the prospect file. Third, you can obtain information on newcomers to your community from many sources. There are subscription services that provide this information, but you might also get it from your local chamber of commerce or utility company. Newcomers are great prospects because their lives are changing, and they may decide to get involved with a church. A fourth way to find a prospect is to do an inside people search. This is a simple procedure in which index cards are passed out to everyone in church. Ask them to give information about anyone they know who does not attend church anywhere. There are many other ways to discover prospects. Train your people to be on the lookout for unchurched people everywhere they go. Anytime they can get at least a name and address, the person they find can be added to the prospect file. One of the most important things a healthy Sunday School does is to continually look for more prospects.

3. *Assign all prospects to the appropriate Sunday School classes.* This has already been mentioned in number one above, but it deserves more emphasis here. Every

member of each prospect family should be assigned to a specific Sunday School class. That class then has the responsibility of reaching out to that prospect. This is one reason why healthy Sunday Schools are age graded. When the Sunday School is properly graded, every prospect that is discovered and added to the prospect file can be easily assigned to a specific class. If, for example, there are four members in a particular prospect family, then as many as four separate classes should be trying to reach members of that family. Any fisherman will tell you that your chances of catching a fish are increased if you have more hooks in the water. By using all of your Sunday School classes to reach out to prospects, you increase the number of "hooks in the water," and increase your chance of reaching people for Jesus Christ.

4. *Teach your members the importance and necessity of outreach.* Model outreach for them and train them how to do it. Teach the Sunday School workers that it is their responsibility to reach out to prospects assigned to their class. This should be addressed as an expectation when Sunday School workers are enlisted; workers should be made to understand that they are expected to participate in outreach. The pastor should preach and teach that all Christians have a responsibility to reach out to others. You cannot expect your members to be faithfully involved in outreach if you haven't taught them that it is their responsibility and duty to God. Tell them what the Bible says about outreach. Let them know that the church will die without outreach. Use testimonies of those who have been reached and of those who have reached others. Talk it up! Expect and encourage participation. Keep it ever before the people.

5. *Select a date and time for organized church wide visitation.* Many churches have abandoned organized visitation, but there is simply no substitute for it. Weekly visitation is best, but if your people are not visiting at all and you can get them going even once a month, that is progress. Church wide visitation may be planned for a weeknight, Sunday afternoon, or Saturday morning, whichever will work best for your church. Visitation time needs to be placed on the church calendar and guarded carefully. Do not place it opposite other events, and do not cancel it very often. Make visitation a regular part of your church's schedule, and encourage the people to attend. Do whatever is necessary to make it a success and an encouraging time. Provide childcare and a meal, if necessary. Most churches need to reach young married couples. The best people to reach out to unchurched

young married couples are the young married couples already in your church. Those who have children can't go visiting if childcare is not provided. A meal may be helpful to those who must come straight to the church from their place of work. In addition to regular weekly visitation, occasionally provide special outreach opportunities. Special emphasis visitation, such as visiting all absentee members or doing a blitz of an entire neighborhood, can also be scheduled.

6. *Make allowances for those who can't participate at the official visitation time.* Regardless of when your visitation time is scheduled, someone will have a conflict. Encourage these members to go visiting on their own, at a time that is more convenient for them. Outreach is a command of the Lord, but everyone may not be able to participate at the "official" church-wide visitation time. Equip your members to understand that church-wide visitation is a component of outreach, but it is not the whole or sole method of outreach.

7. *Organize the visitation area.* This is very important. If possible, provide a table for each Sunday School department or age division. On the tables, place a stack of prospect cards or sheets for each class within that department. Label the table and class stacks clearly, so people won't waste time looking for the appropriate prospect cards. Ideally you should leave the visitation information and materials out all the time so Sunday School workers can access it on Sundays and Wednesdays, as well as at visitation time. If it is not possible to leave the visitation area set up all the time, then put the prospect cards or slips for each class in a folder or binder. Label the folders or binders clearly and put them where they can be easily reached. Remember that people are giving their time to reach out to others, so organize the area so they can quickly and easily get the prospect information they need and get out the door.

8. *Provide materials for those who will go visiting.* Set up a table with all the materials to be used while visiting. The table should include a supply of gospel tracts, flyers about the church, New Testaments to give away, Sunday School curriculum, maps, and door hangers. Door hangers are cards designed to go over a doorknob, on which you can write a note to prospects who are not at home. Also include informational flyers about upcoming events such as revivals, concerts, and Vacation Bible School. Those who go visiting should leave printed materials with the prospects. Printed materials serve as a continuing reminder of

your visit, as well as of the prospect's need for Christ and His church. Keep your material table well stocked.

9. *At visitation time, be upbeat, positive, and encouraging.* Help your members pair up into teams, and give them any necessary instructions. Be brief. Thank them for coming, encourage and motivate them in their efforts, offer to help with directions and other information, then pray and begin making visits. Don't let people stay at the church for a long time. You can't actually do outreach until you get out of the church. Your goal at visitation time is to get the people out of the building and on their way to where the prospects are located. Be sure to set a good example by going out on visitation yourself. Records are very important for evaluation, encouragement, and motivation. Report to the church each week how many were involved in outreach visitation during the previous week. This will serve as a constant reminder and motivator. If possible, create some type of report to show how many people from each Sunday School class were involved in visitation. Since the goal is that every Sunday School class be involved in outreach, such a report will provide praise for those who participate and a reminder for those who don't. Report weekly to the church the number of classes in the Sunday School and the number involved in outreach (which should be at least as many as the number of classes). Be sure that everyone who goes visiting reports the results of their visits on the prospect cards. Information gained from previous visits should be added to the prospect information so future outreachers will know all they can before making additional visits. The ideal arrangement would be to provide a reporting time when everyone returns from visitation. Written reports can be completed and some verbal reports and testimonies shared. This will greatly encourage your people and build a team spirit. Jesus sent out seventy people on visitation (Luke 10:1) and they returned later with joy (Luke 10:17), testifying to one another about the miracles they witnessed on visitation. A reporting time provides an outlet for your people to share the joy of telling others about Jesus Christ.

10. *Encourage Sunday School workers to be "on the lookout" for unchurched people all the time, not just during organized visitation.* The world is full of lost and unchurched people. They are all around you and your church.

> *"Try to develop an outreach consciousness in yourself and in your Sunday School leaders."*

Prospects can be found at the grocery store, the dentist's office, the ballpark, the break room at your place of employment, the school classroom, and in your neighborhood. Look for them constantly, and show genuine concern for them. Invite them to Sunday School, try to get prospect information from them, and even offer to enroll them in your Sunday School. Keep your eyes open for "as you go" prospects and the Lord will bless your efforts.

KEY #9

NEW UNITS ARE CREATED

Unlocking the Purpose of New Units

Several years ago I received a letter from a Georgia Baptist pastor asking for the names of potential candidates for the staff position of Minister of Education. The letter detailed character traits desired, job responsibilities, and benefits offered. I read with interest a statement in the benefits area that indicated that the Minister of Education would receive a monetary bonus for each new teaching unit created. My initial reaction was "you've got to be kidding!" I had never heard of a church responding in such a way. I thought about sending my resume immediately!

After further thought it occurred to me that while the benefit offered was unusual in Southern Baptist circles, this pastor knew what Arthur Flake, J.N. Barnett, Gaines Dobbin, A.V. Washburn, Harry Piland, and Bill Taylor knew and taught. Healthy Sunday Schools and healthy churches create new units.

In the early part of the 20th century, Arthur Flake, in his formula for Sunday School growth spoke of "expanding the organization." In 1953, J.N. Barnette, author of The Pull of the People, wrote:

> "New units grow faster, win more people to Christ, and provide more workers. Fruit comes on new growth. Roses bloom on new growth. Without new growth there would be little fruit for food and few flowers for beauty and perfume. This law is as applicable to Sunday School as to fruit trees."

In 1990, Harry Piland, author of Break Through Sunday School Work, wrote:

> "If Sunday School is to improve, it must change. If it is to grow, it must plan for growth. If it is to achieve BREAKTHROUGH, its organizational structure must be dynamic. Growing Sunday Schools have a growing, expanding organization. They create new classes and departments. They seek out places for new Sunday Schools. They are never satisfied with holding their own. So long as there is one unreached person they will keep reaching out."

In 2001, Bill Taylor and Ken Hemphill, authors of <u>Ten Best Practices To Make Your Sunday School Work</u>, wrote:

> *"Keep clear focus on the purpose of any Bible study group. Sunday School is designed as the foundational strategy for leading persons to faith in the Lord Jesus and building on-mission Christians through open Bible study groups that engage in evangelism, discipleship, ministry, fellowship, and worship. That same purpose is to influence our efforts to multiply leaders and units."*

Are you convinced? Do you believe that creating new units will help you build a healthy Sunday School? Consider why creating new units is a must for building a growing, healthy Sunday School.

Reason #1 – New units produce spiritual growth.
As new leaders are enlisted to create a new unit, the opportunity exists for those leaders to exercise their spiritual gifts, obey the commands of Jesus Christ, and share their personal testimony with individuals who don't know Christ. Spiritual growth occurs.

Reason #2 – New units provide additional opportunities for service and blessing.
New units require committed leaders. They provide places for more people to serve. Some of these leaders may come from other leadership positions in the church, but many will be individuals who currently serve in no ministry. Jethro suggested to his son-in-law, Moses, that additional workers be enlisted to help him in the administration of the Israelite people. Nehemiah enlisted workers to repair the wall of Jerusalem, giving each family a responsibility. New leaders will be blessed as they become a part of an exciting venture of faith.

Reason #3 - New units often produce numerical growth.
New units do not guarantee numerical growth but rather position a church to reach more people and to grow numerically. Some new units fail, but most will grow quickly. New units work harder and are more motivated to aggressively reach out to the lost and unchurched. They invite more prospective members, attempt to enroll more new members, and follow-up more consistently with absentees than older, more established classes. New units put more people to work. New units reach new people.

Reason #4 – New units create a sense of excitement and accomplishment.
Just as the birth of a new baby brings joy and happiness to new parents, so the creation of a new teaching unit brings excitement and joy to the staff and leaders who are involved in the birthing process. This joy has a way of spreading to older, existing classes. For those existing classes that birth a new unit there is a sense of accomplishment that goes with carrying out the Great Commission. New units keep the Sunday School alive and vibrant.

Reason #5 – New units enlarge the organizational base of the Sunday School and provide choices.
People today desire options and choices. New units provide choices for members and prospects alike in the areas of class size, age range, teaching style and curriculum.

Reason #6 – New units can help in meeting the felt needs of individuals.
Through the creation of new units that focus on a particular curriculum or topic, the felt needs of some individuals can be met. As someone once said, we can "scratch their itch."

Reason #7 – New units are more "user friendly" to prospects.
New units are more likely to work at building relationships with prospective members. They are more conscious of the need to assimilate individuals into the life and ministry of the class. They want individuals to fit in and feel like they are a part of the class.

Reason #8 – New units provide an opportunity for absentees and restless members to make a fresh start.
In today's church, individuals at times become dissatisfied with a particular teaching style or curriculum offered. They also may become discouraged by the direction of a class's ministry, or in some other way restless in their involvement with a particular Sunday School class. New units provide an opportunity for these individuals to make a fresh start or meet a perceived need in their life without personal embarrassment or hurt to the existing class.

Reason #9 – New units increase a church's effectiveness in reaching people and teaching the Bible.
New units help keep classes small enough for meaningful Bible study and effective ministry. Effective classes must be aware of the ministry needs of class members and see that these needs are met.

Finding the Right Combination

"Every church that desires to have a healthy Sunday School organization should have an intentional, ongoing plan for creating new units."

This plan requires:

- communication of the overall mission of the Sunday School and of the need for new units.
- complete support of the pastor and staff.
- support from existing classes in birthing new units.
- a belief that every believer is a minister and is to use their spiritual giftedness to advance the mission of the church.
- a belief that every member and prospect should be in a weekly Bible study group.
- a "potential leader" training program that challenges members to identify their spiritual giftedness and explore their leadership potential.
- a "potential leader" training program that guides members toward specific areas of service.

Ken Hemphill and Bill Taylor, in <u>Ten Best Practices To Make Your Sunday School Work</u>, give the following suggestions as to when a church should create new units: (Keep in mind that these numbers are Hemphill's and Taylor's recommendations and should be viewed as general rules of thumb rather than laws.)

Create a New Preschool Class or Department When:
- Birth through age 5 are all in one class or department;
- Babies are in the same department with other ages;
- Kindergartners are in the same department with other ages;
- Class or department of younger preschoolers has 12 or more enrolled;
- Class or department of threes, fours, and pre-K has more than 16 enrolled;
- Class or department of kindergartners has more than 20 enrolled;
- Class or department where only "babysitting" is done;
- More prospects than preschoolers are enrolled.

Create a New Children's Class or Department When:
- Grades 1 through 6 are in one class or department;
- Grade 1 is in a class or department with another grade;

- Grade 6 is in a class or department with another grade;
- Class or department has more than 30 enrolled;
- Class or department has less than 60 percent of enrollment attending;
- A school grade has prospects but none attending.

Create a New Youth Class or Department When:
- All youth are in one class or department;
- More than 60 youth are enrolled in one department;
- More than 12 youth are enrolled in a class;
- A school grade has prospects but little or no attendance;
- Class or department has less than 50 percent enrollment attending;
- A school grade has more prospects than youth enrolled.

Create a New Adult Class When:
- Classes cover too wide of an age span (more than 10 years);
- More than 25 are enrolled in the class;
- Room in which the class meets is often filled;
- Single adult prospects but no single adult class provided;
- Young adult prospects but no class provided;
- Adult prospects in a particular age segment but no class provided;
- Unenrolled adult church members;
- Classes have more prospects than members;
- Classes have more absentees than members present.

Consider these further suggestions:
- Create a new unit in an age division that is experiencing little or no numerical growth.
- Create a new unit in age divisions where needs are not being met.
- Create a new unit when an existing class develops problems in its fellowship or ceases to adequately care for its members.
- Create a new unit when a competent leader is identified who has a passion for starting a class.
- Create a new unit when a special target group exists but no class is currently provided.
- Create new units when the church completes a building program, begins multiple schools, reorganizes the existing school, or in some way acquires additional space.

Breaking Through: How Healthy Sunday Schools Utilize New Units

Does the thought of creating new units scare you? Are you like many Pastors, Ministers of Education, age division staff members, Sunday School Directors, Adult Division Directors, Department Directors, class directors, and teachers who balk at creating new units because of the fear of resistance and the hard work involved? Do you fear resistance that comes from individuals who want to hold on to a particular classroom or relationship with a particular teacher? Do you prefer the easier, more comfortable approach of allowing your Sunday School to drift along year by year without stirring up trouble? This is the attitude of many leaders! The problem with that approach is that the Sunday School is probably not reaching out to lost persons, effectively teaching as many people as possible, or growing numerically. You must ask yourself, "Is the Great Commission of Jesus Christ being carried out as effectively as possible?"

New units can be created in several ways. Following are some ways to create new units as well as steps to take in creating these new units to lessen the resistance from your people and ultimately lead to health in your Sunday School.

1. **The "restructured" class/department**: An existing class or department may be restructured to form two teaching units. For example, a single department for ninth and tenth graders may become two separate departments, one for ninth graders and one for tenth graders. A word of caution: always use the term "birth" or "restructure" rather than "divide" or "split" when utilizing this approach.

2. **The "missionary" class**: An existing class commits to send out a core group of its members to birth a new class. Members sent out may include the teacher and leadership team for the new class.

3. **The "seed" class**: A leadership team and individuals are selected from several existing classes to form the nucleus for a new class.

4. **The "scratch" class**: A leadership team accepts the responsibility and challenge of starting a new class with only a list of prospects.

5. **The "absentee" class**: A leadership team accepts the responsibility and challenge

of starting a new class from a list of Sunday School dropouts and/or irregular attendees.

6. **The "unreached people group" class**: A leadership team accepts the responsibility of starting a new class that targets a specific group of people in the community that the church is not currently reaching. For example, a church may begin a class for a particular ethnic group in the community.

7. **The "nontraditional" class**: A leadership team accepts the responsibility of reaching out to a group of people who will not or cannot attend Bible study at the church facility on Sunday morning. Such groups may include:
   - Weekend workers (policemen, nurses, department store clerks, etc.)
   - Shut-ins
   - Shift workers
   - Businessmen who travel on the weekends
   - People in life-transition stages (new parents, empty nesters, divorcees, re-married, widowed, college students, etc.)
   - Different ethnicities or other language groups

These groups may meet in homes, apartments, office complexes, residential institutions (assisted living homes, nursing homes), etc.

8. **The "elective" class**: A teacher leads a short-term study of a particular curriculum piece focused on meeting a particular need with the goal of transitioning the group reached into an ongoing class. For example, a class on parenting is offered for 13 weeks at which time the participants are encouraged to stay together and begin the study of a new curriculum.

The process for successfully creating new units with minimal resistance from your members includes the following steps:

Step #1– Research.
Study and evaluate the current organization. Research enrollment, average attendance, age breakdowns, prospects available, and growth patterns for the past five years of your Sunday School. Today's computers can make this easy. The data obtained will reveal growth patterns and areas of need.

Step #2– Pray.
Ask God to reveal the areas of greatest need and to provide the leadership needed.

Step #3– Educate.
Help your staff, leaders, and members know why the creation of new units is so important. Leading adults to understand the reasons for organizational changes and expansion will make them less resistant to creating new units. Over an extended period of time, teach growth principles. Encourage dialogue, discussion, input, frank conversation, group decision making, and freedom of choice.

Step #4– Plan.
After examining the current organization and teaching the principles of growth you are ready to make a decision about how many new units can be created. The planning phase must include:

a. *Decide on a time frame for starting the new unit.*
   New units can be started anytime, but the most effective times are the beginning of the new Sunday School year and the beginning of the calendar year in January. During these time periods attendance is higher and more consistent, individuals are more receptive to change and new organizational patterns, re-commitments to Bible study and worship are made, and fewer distractions and disruptions occur.

b. *Determine a possible meeting or classroom place.*

c. *Determine the number and types of leaders needed.*

d. *Select a target group.*
   In selecting these groups consider such factors as gender, age range, grade in school, marital status, and life status.

Allow adequate time for the planning phase. Strive to allow at least six months. As leaders and members become accustomed to organizational changes and realize that creating new units works, additional units can be created with greater frequency and less promotion and communication.

Step #5 – Implement.
The implementation phase should include:

a. *Provide a support system.*
New units must have support. This support may come in the form of a sponsoring class, staff encouragement, prayer group, or ministry team.

b. *Select a team of leaders.*
Enlist the teacher first, then add a class director/coordinator, and at least four prospective members. Co-ed classes and classes for single adults may require a larger leadership team for a successful start. Leaders of the new unit should be experienced Sunday School members capable of building the new unit and passionate about their role in the building process.

c. *Train the leaders.*

d. *Assign a meeting place.*

e. *Provide needed teaching supplies and equipment.*

f. *Select and order curriculum materials.*

g. *Prepare records.*

h. *Contact potential members.*
Class leaders should be encouraged to invite prospective members to be a part of the first class session. Some churches encourage a get-acquainted fellowship several weeks prior to the official start date.

i. *Discover, assign and contact prospects.*
A personal visit, phone call, card, letter, or e-mail message to prospects a week before the official start date will build enrollment and attendance. Some churches may choose to deliver a curriculum piece or study guide.

j. *Publicize the start date.*
Get the word out about the specific date, time, and place the new unit will meet.

Use the church newsletter, order of service, posters, direct mail and e-mail to reach out to potential members.

k. *Plan for and conduct the first session.*
Taylor and Hemphill suggest the following schedule for the first session:
- Party –Provide time for fellowship among leaders, members, and other attendees. Serve light snacks appropriate to the age of the participants. Plan group-building and get-acquainted experiences. Use nametags to help everyone learn names.
- Praise –Ask some leaders and members to tell how God is working in their lives. Do not embarrass new participants, particularly unchurched persons, who may find it awkward to talk about spiritual things. As part of the worship time, read a Psalm or other Scripture passage that will be part of the Bible study for the day. Provide music or lead group singing.
- Prayer –All people have concerns for which they need God's intervention. Some new attendees may not be familiar with the idea of bringing concerns before God confident that He hears, understands, and answers our prayers. As the leadership team learns about individuals in the group, it will become apparent who is comfortable praying aloud in a group. Prayer time can be a vital group-building experience as well as a meaningful time of worship. While this time is important, leaders will want to be sure that plenty of time is allowed for Bible study.
- Participation –Approximately two-thirds of the total session should be designated for Bible teaching.

l. *Evaluate the beginning and follow through.*
Prospects and attendees should be followed up week by week. Write notes of welcome to first time attendees. Encourage regular attendance. Continue to enlist additional class leaders as enrollment grows. Begin care groups to minister to every 4-5 members or couples. Cultivate prospects.

Step #6 – Celebrate.
Report periodically on the progress of the new unit. Provide opportunities for leaders to share a testimony of their experiences. Congratulate leaders for their service and commitment.

Ten Key Ideas That You Can Use

1. Irene Bennett, Minister of Education, of Hillcrest Baptist Church, Savannah, Georgia, created a *Nearly and Newly Wed class* using the curriculum piece, "I Take Thee To Be My Spouse." After enlisting two couples as co-leaders, twenty prospective couples were identified and contacted. The class was successful, reached several new couples for Bible study and active church participation, and produced new leaders for the church.

2. Libby Bridger, Executive Director of Adult Ministries, Hebron Baptist Church, Dacula, Georgia, *encourages existing classes to "birth" new units*. She works through a step-by-step process of meeting with teachers, approaching the sponsoring class, and initiating the new class. Libby wears a scrub suit the day the class is "born." Posters and pink and blue ribbons are displayed throughout the church. A gift is taken into the new class and candy and a birth certificate are presented to the sponsoring class. Libby has detailed her approach in a booklet entitled "Pain Free Delivery for Birthing New Units". She will be happy to share a copy with anyone who is interested.

3. Banks Corl, Minister of Education, Shades Mountain Baptist Church, Birmingham, Alabama, uses a similar *"birthing method."* The process begins with the identification of 6-12 individuals who are willing to move out from the existing class. Six weeks before the start date, each new leader stands before the class and in thirty seconds shares why they believe God is calling them to help start the new class. Other class members are encouraged to join them if they feel led. Behind the scenes, class leaders meet to make sure there is a proper balance in both units. A training session is offered four weeks prior to the start, and a fellowship for prospects and class leaders is held two weeks prior to the start of the new class. The new class is advertised in the church newsletter and bulletin; interested individuals are encouraged to meet the teachers at the greeters' desk. The Sunday before the start of the new class, the sponsoring class has a "baby shower" during the first part of the class period. Gifts such as dry erase markers and an ice bucket are presented and a commissioning prayer is said. The new class begins with a short term, high interest topic then transitions to regular curriculum materials. Jonathan Propes, Minister of Education, Tabernacle Baptist Church, Decatur, Illinois uses the same approach. Throughout his church

pictures of storks are displayed, new births are announced in worship services, and on the first Sunday of the new class the sponsoring class is provided with a cake.

4. *Special Needs classes* are being started in several churches. Groupings include:
   a. hearing impaired
   b. MANKS – married adults no kids
   c. engaged couples
   d. blended families
   e. mentally challenged
   f. single parents

5. Carter Shotwell, Minister of Education, Lake Pointe Church, Rockwall, Texas, begins "*hot topic*" classes three times per year (August, January, and the week after Easter). These classes are four weeks in length and target individuals who are not currently attending a traditional class. Groups with a high affinity (newlyweds, parents of teens, etc.) become traditional classes. Those classes with a "mixed bag" of people are assimilated into new or existing classes. This approach has been very effective in reaching those who have not been attending Bible study.

6. *Elective classes* are being offered in a number of churches as a tool for reaching those persons who don't normally attend Sunday School. Class topics include:
   a. money management
   b. parenting
   c. marriage enrichment
   d. Experiencing God, by Henry Blackaby
   e. Bible study material written by Beth Moore

7. Bill Cole, Associate Pastor, Discipleship and Christian Education, First Baptist Church, Pompano Beach, Florida, has created a class for young adults that meets during the second Sunday School hour. The *class discusses the pastor's sermon and text for the day.* The leaders of the class receive the topic, scripture passage, and sermon outline early in the week in order to prepare questions to "jump start" the discussion. After several weeks there was no need to "jump start" the discussion as class members came to class with their sermon notes ready to discuss.

8. Bob Shelton, Minister to Adults and Singles, Northwest Baptist Church, Oklahoma City, Oklahoma, is in the process of beginning *Bible study groups in homes* in various locations around the city. These groups will meet on Sunday evening, are non-age graded, and will use Serendipity materials.

9. Danny Bennett, Minister of Education, Calvary Baptist Church, Clearwater, Florida, offers *new classes under the heading of "Seasons of Life."* Classes are started for young adults, parents of preschoolers, parents of high school students, 30-somethings, etc. These classes are loosely age graded and utilize LifeWay's "Family Bible Series" curriculum.

10. Jon Breshears, Associate Pastor of Discipleship, First Baptist Church, North Augusta, South Carolina, has begun *creating home Bible study groups in various parts of the community to reach church members not currently in a Sunday School class*. Groups are loosely age graded and meet for approximately three hours. Half of the period is spent in Bible study and the remainder of the time is spent eating and enjoying fellowship. Some groups meet weekly while others meet every other week. A variety of curriculum is being used and must be approved by the Associate Pastor. Existing class members, worship attendees, and unchurched members of the community are being reached. The church is planning to tear down an existing education facility in the near future and is considering changing completely to home studies during the construction of new space.

Appendix

The purpose of the following report is to provide information that may be used to strengthen Georgia Baptist Churches. The Sunday School/Open Group Ministries staff of the Georgia Baptist Convention desires to provide training and resources to enable churches to develop healthy small group (Sunday School) ministries. This information can help you to evaluate and improve the Sunday School ministry of your church.

The churches invited to participate in the survey were among the fifty fastest growing churches in Georgia. The selection of the churches was based both on Sunday School growth and on effectiveness in evangelism. Why was the focus on Sunday School growth? A church that has a growing worship service or a growing membership may or may not have a growing Sunday School, but every church that has a growing Sunday School has a growing worship attendance and a growing membership. A healthy Sunday School ministry impacts all other ministries of the church. Why was effectiveness in evangelism considered in identifying the fastest growing Sunday Schools? Churches that are growing without winning the lost to Christ are simply experiencing transfer growth. The churches participating in this survey tend to have Great Commission Sunday Schools that are winning people to Christ and are assimilating them into the Sunday School.

The criteria for selecting the churches was based on a study of statistics provided to the state convention for the Annual Church Profiles. The growth was assessed for a five-year period comparing the statistics for 1995-2000. Churches were evaluated based on net growth in Sunday School attendance and enrollment, percentage growth in Sunday School attendance and enrollment, total baptisms and baptism ratios. The information on net growth favored larger churches whereas percentage growth and baptism ratios favored smaller churches. The result was a group of fifty of the fastest growing Sunday Schools in Georgia. The churches are located in all regions of Georgia, in all sizes of towns and represent all sizes of churches. Forty percent of the churches were averaging less than 150 in Sunday School five years ago and twenty-one percent were averaging less than 100. The churches spanned all sizes and included the church that has the largest Sunday School in Georgia, which is still continuing to grow. These are not the only churches in Georgia that are experiencing Sunday School growth. Thankfully, several hundred churches have healthy, growing Sunday Schools. How effective have the participating churches been? A study of the 2000 Annual Church Profile revealed that 1.3% of Georgia Baptist churches accounted for 75% of the net gain in enrollment and 42% of the net gain in attendance in Georgia above the previous year.

Forty-six of the fifty churches responded to the survey. They are all listed on the final page of this report. These churches are to be commended for their outstanding growth. The study of a larger number of churches will continue in the future as a broader group of churches are surveyed for comparative analysis. Further information will be published to encourage and strengthen Georgia's Sunday Schools in the coming years.

Where do churches with "non-traditional" small group ministries fit into the survey? This study does not distinguish between small groups, cell groups, Bible Study groups, or traditional Sunday Schools. The principles for leading small group ministries that are effective evangelistically are similar regardless of the time the groups meet or the term used to describe the group. "Sunday School" is the designation used in this report because of its familiarity and prevalence of use among Georgia Baptist churches. Some of the participating churches use terms other than "Sunday School" and meet at times other than Sunday mornings.

Survey Question: Which best describes your Sunday School?
85% - All classes meet on Sunday morning.
11% - All classes meet on Sunday morning with a few exceptions.
4% - There is a blend of Sunday morning classes and weekday cell groups.
0% - Most classes are weekday cell groups with few or no Sunday morning groups.

The survey revealed ten common factors in these churches that related to the growth of their Sunday Schools. The factors are listed and briefly described in order of prevalence on the following pages. The descriptions are followed by a ten-question survey based on the common factors. The final phase of the project was to re-evaluate these forty-six churches based on the concluding survey. The average church included in this study could answer "yes" to 8.6 of the ten questions posed based on these ten common factors. All but two of the churches could answer "yes" to seven or more of the questions. What about the two churches that could answer "yes" to fewer than seven questions? Why are they experiencing growth in the Sunday School? A further review of their surveys revealed that those two churches have experienced phenomenal worship growth that likely accounts for their Sunday School growth. The two combined have only 40% of their worship attendance in Sunday School each week. The average ratio of the participating churches was 72% and the Georgia combined average is 71% of worship attendance in Sunday School. 40% is an unhealthy balance that reflects poor Sunday School practices that are a hindrance to assimilation. These churches have experienced growth in Sunday School but are missing an ideal opportunity to take Bible Study groups and assimilation to a greater level.

Keep the following points in mind as you consider the ten common factors of Georgia's fastest growing Sunday Schools. **First, none of the factors stands alone.** These Sunday Schools are growing because they are doing many things well. The more prevalent factors are in many ways the most essential. The implementation and application of one or two without the others will not be sufficient to prompt or sustain growth. **Second, Sunday School growth takes work**. Yes, it is first and foremost a work of God, but it is also the work of God through His body, the church. The ministry that occurs Monday through Saturday is as essential as the ministry that occurs on Sunday morning. These factors clearly make this point. **Third, each of the participating churches tends to be struggling with one or more of these areas.** Only sixteen of the forty-six churches would be able to say "yes" to all ten of the concluding questions. These churches would humbly admit that they are still struggling with application and implementation in some of these areas. This attitude has been clear in personal interaction with each of the participating churches. These are not perfect churches, but they are churches passionate about reaching their communities and teaching God's Word.

Common Factor One

98% of these churches provide training for their Sunday School Leaders.

The most common factor discovered in the survey related to the training of leaders. All but one of the churches, or 98%, reported that they involve their leaders in training. Could it be that the reason that they are the fastest growing Sunday Schools is because they have trained and skilled leaders? That certainly is at least a portion of the explanation. These churches were of all sizes and in all types of communities and settings. The fact that they train their leaders was one of the most overwhelming common practices related to Sunday School.

Survey Question: Which of the following do you use to train Sunday School leaders?
17% - Weekly workers meetings
 4% - Bi-Weekly workers meetings
63% - Monthly workers meetings
 9% - Quarterly workers meetings
 7% - No regularly scheduled workers meetings

Note that 84% of these churches meet with their leaders for training at least monthly. 93% meet with their leaders at least quarterly. Only three of the forty-six churches do not meet with their leaders on a regular basis. Two of these three churches do provide training for their leaders by other means. Only one of the churches did not specify any method for training their Sunday School leaders. In addition, 92% of the churches that provide training on a regular basis utilize additional opportunities to train their leaders.

Survey Question: Which of the following do you use to train Sunday School leaders?
46% - A launch event in August
46% - An annual teacher appreciation banquet with speaker
41% - Participation in state Sunday School conferences
37% - Participation in associational training
20% - An annual leaders retreat
15% - Participation at Ridgecrest
13% - Special training events/classes in the church
 0% - Other

Summary: These churches have taken the admonition of Ephesians 4:11-16 to heart. They are "equipping the saints for the work of ministry, for the edifying of the body of Christ." They meet regularly with their leaders for inspiration, instruction and accountability and provide a variety of training opportunities in addition to regularly scheduled training to encourage their leaders to be the best ministers possible as they serve Christ through the Sunday School ministry. 80% of these churches either require or strongly urge their leaders to participate in training (See Common Factor Nine for more details).

Common Factor Two

96% of these churches believe that the Pastor's support of the Sunday School is important or very important to the health of their church.

Survey Question: How important do you think the following are to the health of your church?

	VERY IMPORTANT	IMPORTANT	FAIRLY IMPORTANT	NOT IMPORTANT
Pastor's Support of S.S.	87%	9%	4%	0%

Pastors with the attitude that they are "just not Sunday School [people]" are unlikely to have churches that experience the type of growth found in these surveyed churches. The Pastors in these churches tend to be those that believe that Sunday School is critical to outreach, assimilation, spiritual growth and ministry in their churches. The Pastor may or may not be directly involved in the administration of the Sunday School, but he is the key communicator of the value and importance of Sunday School in his church.

Survey Question: Who is the key administrative leader of the Sunday School?
63% - The Minister of Education (full-time)
18% - The Pastor (full-time)
13% - A volunteer Sunday School director
4% - The Minister of Education (bi-vocational)
0% - The Pastor (bi-vocational)
2% - Other (The Administrative Pastor)

82% of these churches have someone other than the Pastor providing direct leadership over the Sunday School ministry. Yet they are clear that the Pastor's support is critical to their success. The Pastors in these churches tend to be the key leader or the chief "cheerleader" for the Sunday School ministry.

Note that 100% of the churches have someone who is assigned responsibility for leadership of the Sunday School ministry. Every church identified a specific person as the administrative leader– most commonly a full-time Minister of Education.

KEY Strategies - FOR HEALTHY SUNDAY SCHOOLS

It is advantageous to have a full-time Minister of Education on the church staff, but that fact alone does not guarantee the growth of the Sunday School–though it should. A more important conclusion is that a church does not require a full-time Minister of Education in order to experience growth. 37% of the churches surveyed do not have a full-time Minister of Education yet are among the fifty fastest growing Sunday Schools in Georgia.

Summary: These churches have someone who takes responsibility for the leadership of the Sunday School ministry. The Pastor is involved in providing direct leadership or key support for the person assigned this responsibility. His support is viewed as critical to the success of the Sunday School in these churches.

Common Factor Three

96% of these churches are overcoming space limitations.

These churches have overcome barriers that come with limited space. They have developed and implemented strategies that enable them to move beyond 80% of capacity. The quality and quantity of space are important to the health and growth of the church. Many of these churches might experience greater growth if more space were available. However, they are not waiting on the completion of a future construction project in order to continue their growth. Their approach to and creative use of space reflects a "whatever it takes" attitude on the part of the congregation towards reaching their community with the gospel. Over one-fourth reported that construction of new facilities is underway. 96% are completely out of space in Sunday School, but they are still growing. Why? Because they discover and utilize other options in order to continue growing.

Survey Question: Which of the following are you using to create space for Sunday School?
59% - Multiple Sunday Schools (two, three, or more hours)
39% - Multiple classes in large areas (such as a gym or fellowship hall without walls)
28% - New space currently under construction
26% - Off-campus during Sunday morning
24% - Mobile units
 9% - Classes meeting other than Sunday morning on campus

7% - Other (Including sanctuary class, hallways, workrooms, offices, a purchased house, Wednesday night S.S.)
2% - Groups in homes (cell groups)

Notice that the number of churches using Mobile Units is similar to the number with space under construction. The members make sacrifices by meeting in less desirable settings if needed in order to sustain growth. The focus is on reaching the community. Schedules and room assignments are not held sacred in these churches. People are willing to change rooms, locations and meeting times in order for more people to be reached for Christ and included in Bible Study. Although they exceed the capacity of their space they continue to grow. These churches are also dealing with overcrowded worship space. 72% of these churches have addressed this challenge by hosting multiple worship services on Sunday.

Summary: The rapid growth of the Sunday School in these churches has caused the facilities to be used beyond capacity. The staff and members of these churches have determined not to allow space to deter them from continued growth. They address this challenge by using the space for more than one hour on Sunday morning as well as by seeking creative ways to expand space until a construction project can be completed. They have overcome space limitations and continue to grow despite the difficulty of meeting in overgrown space.

Common Factor Four

91% of these churches practice "open enrollment."

These churches do not make it difficult to join a Sunday School class. They understand that membership in a class is not the equivalent of membership in the church. They tend to be aggressive in enrolling new members and prospects in Bible Study groups. 9% of the churches have a *closed enrollment* policy. They require that a person attend several times in a row before enrolling and/or drop those from the roll that are absent for an extended period. How can they grow with a *closed enrollment*? The reason is because they are doing so many other things so well. Their aggressiveness in evangelism and ministry results in a push forward in enrollment despite a *closed enrollment* policy. This may be a limiting factor though they are experiencing growth. 74% of these churches practice *unlimited open enrollment.* **They will enroll**

anyone, anywhere, at any time so long as the person agrees. A person may enroll before they even visit. Additionally, a person is not removed from the roll unless they die, move, join another church or request to be removed. They make it easy to get on the Sunday School roll and difficult to be removed! 17% of these churches have a *limited open enrollment* practice. They either require that a person attend before enrolling or remove those from the roll that are absent for an extended period. They are not necessarily aggressive about enrolling nor are they resistant once a person visits or joins. The aggressiveness of these churches towards enrollment also appears to result in more of their members receiving ministry through the Sunday School. Their enrollment essentially serves as a ministry list.

What is the percentage of Sunday School enrollment to resident membership for these 46 churches? **92%**
How does this compare to all GBC churches combined? **70%** (2000 ACP)

These *open enrollment* practices are also reflected in the approach to those who join the church by baptism or transfer of membership.

Survey Question: How do you address the enrollment of new church members?
43% - They are strongly encouraged to enroll when they join.
41% - They are automatically enrolled when they join
 4% - They cannot enroll until they attend a class.
 4% - We are passive about enrolling new members.

How does the more aggressive approach impact their percentages? The motivation to purge Sunday School rolls is often to increase the percentage of attendance to enrollment. In reality there is not a major difference. These Sunday Schools averaged 46% of their enrollment in attendance each Sunday. All GBC churches combined averaged 49% (2000 ACP) of their enrollment in attendance each week. These churches that tend to be more aggressive in enrollment affected the percentage of enrolled members present only slightly. This lower percentage is also a reflection of the more aggressive approach.

Summary: These churches have a growing enrollment and an open enrollment practice.

Common Factor Five

85% of these churches are using an evangelistic training process or method.

The first common factor addressed the issue of Sunday School leader training. That is not where equipping begins or ends in these churches. It takes an average of thirty-nine members to lead a person to Christ in a Southern Baptist Church in a given year. The average in the Georgia Baptist Convention is thirty-seven members to lead a person to Christ. These churches all have lower than average ratios in this regard. These forty-six churches accounted for 15% of Georgia's baptisms according to the 2000 Annual Church Profile. Common Factor Five shows that these churches tend to use strategies or programs as a training point to lead their members to become involved and effective in personal evangelism.

Survey Question: Which of the following evangelism training processes and/or methods are currently being utilized in your church?
46% - FAITH
17% - Sharing Jesus Without Fear
15% - One-day soul winning workshops
15% - None
13% - The Net
9% - C.W.T.
9% - Other (Becoming a Contagious Christian, Soul Winning Classes)
4% - Evangelism Explosion

Note that the numbers add up to greater than 100% indicating that some of the churches utilize more than one training process or method. 12% of Georgia Baptist churches are currently certified in the FAITH Evangelism and Sunday School strategy. By contrast 46% of the fastest growing churches (Sunday Schools) are using FAITH for training their staff and members in evangelism. The key is not "the" training process or strategy used by these churches. The key is that there is "a" strategy used to train and motivate leaders to be involved in personal evangelism.

Summary: These churches are intentional in training their leaders and members in personal evangelism. They use a variety of methods with FAITH evangelism being the most predominant strategy. Their assertiveness in evangelism training results in more baptisms than the average church experiences. This feeds the growth of the Sunday School that in turn provides an avenue of assimilation and introductory Bible Studies for new believers in all age groups.

Common Factor Six

83% of these churches are creating new units.

The participating churches completed the survey two months before the beginning of the new Sunday School year. 83% of these churches already knew that they would be starting new classes in the fall and were able to specify how many units they planned to create. The percentage involved in creating new units was higher when giving consideration to those churches that started new classes in the previous nine months.

79% started one or more units in the previous nine months and were planning to start one or more units as the new "Sunday School year" began.

4% started one or more units in the previous nine months but had no definite plans to start a new unit when the new "Sunday School year" began.

4% did not start a new unit in the past nine months but were planning to create one or more units when the new "Sunday School year" began.
13% did not start a new unit in the past nine months and had no definite plans to start a new unit when the new "Sunday School year" began.

Was the creation of new units a response to the growth of the Sunday School or one of the causes of the exceptional growth?

Survey Question: Which best describes your approach to new units?
54% - We are intentional in the creation of new units as a growth strategy.
37% - We create new units as needed.
7% - We create new units when suggested by individual classes.
2% - We avoid the creation of new units.

Over half of the churches create new units as a growth strategy. The others are starting units in response to growth. They also are receiving the benefits of birthing new classes. The benefits are two-fold. First, new classes tend to grow faster than established classes. Second, the creation of new units affects the attitude of the congregation. Common Factor Three addressed the fact that these churches are overcoming space limitations. This is indicative of churches that have a "whatever it takes" attitude. Churches that create new classes have established a "missionary" attitude. To leave an established class where a comfort zone has been established requires a "missionary" attitude on the part of the members. Common Factor One noted that these churches train their leaders. There is also a connection between the training factor and the factor of creating new units. A trained teacher understands that a growing enrollment and the birthing of new classes is critical to the health of a growing Sunday School. They are unselfish and see the creation of new classes as a compliment, rather than a threat, to their leadership.

Summary: These churches are starting new units to broaden the base for prospective growth. Instead of being resistant, they embrace the opportunity that growth brings and the "missionary" attitude that it creates.

Common Factor Seven

80% of these churches have a weekly visitation ministry.

The fact that these churches are experiencing such outstanding growth in the Sunday School implies that they are all engaged in effective outreach. The other 20% of these churches are involved in outreach and evangelism though they do not have an established "weekly" visitation ministry. Common Factor Five addressed their use of evangelistic strategies and methods for training their leaders. This factor points out that the training is wedded to practical application. This is not to suggest that visitation is the sole application. However, purposefully meeting each week to go to homes in order to share Christ, visit prospects and make ministry visits to absentees sets the tone for the entire congregation. Does visitation still work? The fact that these churches are so effective points to the fact that visitation can work and that it does play a role in the growth of the Sunday School.

Survey Question: Does your church have a weekly visitation?
80% - Yes
20% - No

Their visitation involves other leaders in addition to the Pastor and staff. The churches were asked how many people they average at visitation each week. This number was compared to the number of classes/units that the churches have. The average at visitation was one person for every two classes. As an example, a church with twenty classes was averaging ten at weekly visitation. Note that this is an average ratio indicating that half of the churches had a greater average attendance.

Scheduled visitation is not the only way that these churches maintain contact with prospects and absentees. These churches also expect their leaders and class members to contact, follow-up and minister to people throughout the week.

Survey Question: Are classes expected to report contacts on records each week?
61% - Yes
39% - No

All of the churches are effective in engaging the congregation and leaders to invite guests. Note that most of the churches provide motivation and light accountability by having the classes report the total contacts made each Sunday. This would have been Factor Eleven if the list had been extended.

Summary: These churches schedule a time each week for the staff and the Sunday School members to meet for the purpose of visiting the homes of prospects and members. Visitation includes class members as well as professional staff. Leaders and class members alike are expected to make contacts throughout the week and to report these each Sunday for the purpose of accountability and in order to measure progress.

Common Factor Eight

78% of these churches have a prospect list.

These churches intentionally identify people that are not active in Sunday School, are not involved in a church, and are non-believers. Common Factor Seven revealed that a majority of these churches have structured weekly visitation. Members do not show up each week confused about where they are to go and what they are to do. Prospects have been identified to give direction to visitation, evangelism and ministry contacts. Consider the old saying: "If you aim at nothing you will hit it every time."

These churches are growing because they have identified a target. The targets are those who are in need of a relationship with Christ and those that are not presently active in church. This factor connects with most, if not all, of the others. The Sunday School does not exist for the members alone. *Sunday School is the foundational strategy in a local church for leading people to faith in the Lord Jesus Christ and for building Great Commission Christians through Bible Study Groups that engage people in evangelism, discipleship, fellowship, ministry and worship* (from Sunday School for a New Century). The churches identify and gather information on prospects including their names, ages, addresses, phone numbers and spiritual condition. Evaluating spiritual condition includes identifying their level of church involvement and their personal relationship with Christ. They are then assigned to visitation teams and/or Sunday School classes for follow-up and ministry.

Survey Question: Does your Sunday School have a prospect list?
78% - Yes
22% - No

The average number of prospects per church was also identified. This was compared with the enrollment of the church. The average prospect list in these churches contained the equivalent of 46% of the number enrolled in the Sunday School. These churches also have an average attendance of 46% of enrollment each Sunday. In other words, their prospect list was equal to the number that they averaged in Sunday School each week. For example: for every 100 people in Sunday School there were 100 prospects identified and on the prospect list.

Summary: These churches are intentional in identifying prospects. These include people–believers and unbelievers– that are not affiliated with or active in another church or Sunday School. These people are identified and placed on a list or in a file for purposes of ministry and follow-up. The lists include a number of names equal to the average Sunday School attendance.

Common Factor Nine

78% of these churches have high standards for their leaders.

These churches do not shy away from communicating high expectations to their leaders. 78% of these churches utilize *leadership commitments or leadership covenants.*

20% provide *general guidelines* for their leaders. These are provided as part of the enlistment or re-enlistment process. Only one of the churches did not address expectations in any formal or informal manner. Higher expectations can be successfully implemented and do impact the effectiveness and health of Sunday School.

Survey Question: Which of the following would be most true of your expectation of leaders?
43% - Leaders sign a covenant that outlines expectations.
35% - Expectations are clearly communicated, but no covenant is signed.
20% - Expectations are known, but not specifically communicated.
 2% - Expectations are not addressed in any formal or informal manner.

General Guidelines are written or verbally communicated standards or expectations of teachers and other leaders. The leaders do not make a specific commitment, but they do understand what the expectations are. 20% of the churches take this approach.

Leadership Commitments are written standards and expectations to which a leader agrees at the beginning of the "Sunday School year." This is a verbal or "handshake" agreement between the leader and the church. 35% of the churches take this approach.

Leadership Covenants are written standards and expectations to which a leader agrees and commits by signing a covenant with the church. 43% of the churches take this approach. 78% of the churches ask their leaders to make either a verbal or a signed commitment to fulfill their responsibilities. These churches expect leaders to participate in training.

Survey Question: How would you best characterize expectations of leaders with regard to training?
52% - We strongly urge leaders to participate in training.
28% - We require participation in training.
17% - We encourage, but do not require, participation in training.
 2% - We do not provide training.

80% of the churches strongly urge or require participation in training. This would relate to Common Factor One. These churches provide training for their Sunday School leaders. The training is provided and the leaders are expected to participate in order to enhance teaching skills and to grow in their leadership.

Summary: These churches communicate expectations and standards to their leaders. The leaders agree to serve according to these expectations. Participation in training is strongly urged or required of the leaders. The result is that leaders develop a greater level of skill and a deeper level of commitment that impacts the growth of the Sunday School.

Common Factor Ten

78% of these churches intentionally organize the Sunday School for growth.

Survey Question: Do you intentionally organize classes for growth?
78% - Yes
22% - No

This point is connected to Common Factor Six. These churches are creating new units. Intentionally organizing for growth is done with the assumption that classes will outgrow space or will outgrow the ability to maintain the same level of ministry and will then need to birth a new class. This purposeful organization is reflected by, though not limited to, the following ways.

1- There are multiple leaders enlisted to serve in each class.
What was the ratio of Sunday School leaders to units? 3:1

Notice that classes had an average of three leaders. These leaders include a variety of roles in addition to that of "teacher." A team can accomplish together more than a teacher can accomplish alone.

2- There are assigned leadership roles in addition to that of "teacher."
Survey Question: What Sunday School leaders are present in your Adult Sunday School classes? (some churches did not answer this question – numbers may be lower than actual)
91% - Teacher
74% - Care Group Leaders
67% - Class Secretary
59% - Outreach Leader
17% - Apprentice/Co-teacher
17% - Prayer Coordinator

15% - Fellowship Coordinator
20% - Other (Greeter, Class Coordinators, FAITH leader, etc.)

<u>3- The classes are age graded.</u>
Survey Question: Which best reflects the way your adult classes are organized?
87% - "Most" classes are co-ed
50% - Classes are only loosely age graded
33% - Classes are tightly age graded
4% - A structure other than age grading is employed
4% - "Most" classes are all male or all female
2% - "All" classes are men's classes or women's classes

Summary: The classes are organized for growth. Multiple leaders are enlisted for and within each class to meet ministry goals and needs. They tend to be co-ed, age graded classes. This provides for affinity, assimilation and accountability in all age groups.

EFFECTIVE SUNDAY SCHOOLS COMMON FACTORS SURVEY

QUESTION:		
Does your church provide training for the Sunday School leaders?	Yes	No
Does the Pastor provide leadership and/or support for the Sunday School?	Yes	No
Does the congregation have an attitude of flexibility about the schedule and use of space?	Yes	No
Does your church intentionally enroll new people and practice "open enrollment?"	Yes	No
Does your church use and apply an evangelistic training method or process?	Yes	No
Is your church receptive to and active in creating new classes?	Yes	No
Does your church have a weekly visitation and outreach night?	Yes	No
Does your church have an active prospect list?	Yes	No
Do the Sunday School leaders in your church make formal or informal commitments when enlisted to serve?	Yes	No
Are your classes intentionally organized for the purpose of ministry and growth?	Yes	No
TOTAL		

*Georgia's fastest growing Sunday Schools could answer "yes" to an average of 8.6 of these questions. 96% answered yes to seven or more.

Answered Yes
9-10 Excellent
 7-8 Good
 5-6 Fair

EFFECTIVE SUNDAY SCHOOLS COMMON FACTORS SURVEY
For Individual Sunday School Classes

QUESTION:		
Does your class encourage participation and provide training for the Sunday School class leaders?	Yes	No
Is the teacher purposeful and active in leading the class to grow and supportive of the growth goals of the church?	Yes	No
Does your class have an attitude of flexibility about the schedule and use of space?	Yes	No
Does your class intentionally enroll new people and practice "open enrollment?"	Yes	No
Does your class and the class leadership use and participate in an evangelistic training method or process?	Yes	No
Is your class receptive to and active in creating new classes?	Yes	No
Does your class participate in the weekly visitation and outreach night?	Yes	No
Does your class have an active and up-to-date prospect list?	Yes	No
Do your class leaders make formal or informal commitments when enlisted to serve?	Yes	No
Is your class intentionally organized for the purpose of growth and ministry?	Yes	No
TOTAL		

Answered Yes
9-10 Excellent
 7-8 Good
 5-6 Fair

KEY Strategies - FOR HEALTHY SUNDAY SCHOOLS

CHURCH	ASSOCIATION	
Atco Baptist Church, Cartersville	Bartow	Wayne Hamrick, Pastor
Bethlehem First Baptist Church, Bethlehem	Appalachee	Jody Hice, Pastor
Blackshear Place Baptist Church, Flowery Branch	Chattahoochee	George Barnett, Interim
Braelinn Baptist Church, Peachtree City	Fairburn	Keith Moore, Pastor
Cascade Hills Baptist Church, Columbus	Columbus	William Purvis, Pastor
Center Hill Baptist Church, Loganville	Gwinnett Metro	David Dills, Pastor
Chestnut Mountain Baptist Church, Flowery Branch	Chattahoochee	Jeff Benefield, Pastor
Chicopee Baptist Church, Gainesville	Chattahochee	Mike Gilleland, Assoc Pastor
Conyers First Baptist Church, Conyers	Stone Mountain	Paul Purvis, Pastor
Dayspring Baptist Church, Byron	Rehoboth	Chad Everson, Pastor
Douglasville First Baptist Church, Douglasville	West Metro	John Pennington, Pastor
Eagle's Landing First Baptist Church, McDonough	Henry	Timothy Dowdy, Pastor
Emmanuel Baptist Church, Blackshear	Piedmont-Okefenokee	Don Hattaway, Pastor
Emmanuel Baptist Church, Springfield	Savannah	Roland Dann, co pastor
Emmanuel Baptist Church, Springfield	Savannah	Alfred Smith, co pastor
Faith Baptist Church, Chatsworth	Murray	Vince Goble, Pastor
Faith Baptist Church, Monroe	Appalachee	Chris Conner, Pastor
Fellowship Baptist Church, Brinson	Bowen	Stanley Phillips, Pastor
Gatlin Creek Baptist Church, Thomasville	Thomas	Don Prevatt, Pastor
Greenforest Community Baptist Church, Decatur	Atlanta	George McCalep, Pastor
Hebron Baptist Church, Dacula	Mulberry	Larry Wynn, Pastor
Hopewell Baptist Church, Gainesville	Chattahoochee	Robert Foster, Pastor
Johns Creek Baptist Church, Alpharetta	Atlanta	William Self, Pastor
Johnson Ferry Baptist Church, Marietta	Noonday	Bryant Wright, Pastor
Leesburg First Baptist Church, Leesburg	Mallary	Bobby Harrell, Pastor
Loganville First Baptist Church, Loganville	Gwinnett Metro	Ronald Kendall, Pastor
Maynard Baptist Church, Forsyth	Centennial	Lee Marvin, Pastor
Midway Macedonia Baptist Church, Carrollton	Carrollton	Todd Wright, Pastor
Mt Pleasant Baptist Church, Carrollton	Carrollton	Douglas New, Pastor
New Life Baptist Church, Adel	Valdosta	Harris Whitman, Pastor
North Metro First Baptist Church, Lawrenceville	Gwinnett Metro	Frank Cox, Pastor
Northside Baptist Church, Valdosta	Valdosta	Kenneth Hall, Pastor
Norwich Baptist Church, Brunswick	Southeast	David Stokes, Pastor
Oak Hill Baptist Church, Griffin	Flint River	Steve Steward, Pastor
Pleasant Grove Baptist Church, Hiram	West Metro	Quinn Evans, Pastor
Richmond Hill First Baptist Church, Richmond Hill	Savannah	Michael Lewis, Pastor
Riverbend Baptist Church, Gainesville	Chattahoochee	Harry Kennedy, Pastor
Second Baptist Church, Warner Robins	Rehoboth	Rastus Salter, Pastor
Shirley Hills Baptist Church, Warner Robins	Rehoboth	Andy Cook, Pastor
Summit Baptist Church, Loganville	Appalachee	Carl Butcher, Pastor
Sunrise Baptist Church, Lawrenceville	Gwinnett Metro	David Poe, Pastor
Warren Baptist Church, Augusta	Augusta	Charles Clark, SS Dir
West Cobb Baptist Church, Powder Springs	Noonday	Ken Williams, Pastor
Wildwood First Baptist Church, Acworth	Noonday	Russ Shinpoch, Pastor
Woodstock First Baptist Church, Woodstock	Noonday	Johnny Hunt, Pastor
Woolsey Baptist Church, Fayetteville	Flint River	Charles Chambers, Pastor
Zion Baptist Church, Braselton	Mulberry	Mike Phillips, Pastor